Two Views of the Fort Dearborn Massacre

Two Views of the Fort Dearborn Massacre

The Potawatomi Indians & the U.S. Army
During the War of 1812

The Fort Dearborn Massacre

Linai T. Helm

and

The Story of Old Fort Dearborn
(Extract)

J. Seymour Currey

LEONAUR

Two Views of the Fort Dearborn Massacre
The Potawatomi Indians & the U.S. Army During the War of 1812
The Fort Dearborn Massacre
by Linai T. Helm
and
The Story of Old Fort Dearborn (extract)
by J. Seymour Currey

First published under the titles
The Fort Dearborn Massacre
and
The Story of Old Fort Dearborn (extract)

Leonaur is an imprint
of Oakpast Ltd

ISBN: 978-1-78282-072-7 (hardcover)
ISBN: 978-1-78282-073-4 (softcover)

http://www.leonaur.com

Publisher's Notes

The views expressed in this book are not necessarily
those of the publisher.

Contents

The Fort Dearborn Massacre

Contents

To my Native City
Chicago
Whose Marvellous Growth and Development
I Have Watched With Pride and Unfailing
Interest Since the Year 1835
I Dedicate This Book

Introduction

The narrative of Lieutenant Linai T. Helm, one of the two officers who survived the Chicago Massacre, mysteriously disappeared nearly one hundred years ago. This manuscript has lately been found and is now in the possession of the Michigan Pioneer and Historical Society, by whose kind permission it is here presented to the public, together with letters explaining its loss and its recovery. It is the earliest extant account given by a participator in the fearful tragedy of August 15, 1812. It was written by Lieutenant Helm in 1814, at the request of Judge Augustus B. Woodward, of Detroit, and was accompanied by a letter asking Judge Woodward's opinion as to whether the strictures made in the narrative upon the conduct of Captain Heald would result in Helm's being court-martialled for disrespect to his commanding officer.

Judge Woodward evidently advised Lieutenant Helm not to take the risk, for the manuscript was found many years later among the Judge's papers. That Lieutenant Helm was a soldier rather than a scholar is evidenced by the faulty construction of his narrative. Its literary imperfections, however, in no way detract from its value as a truthful account of the events he describes.

In the records of the Michigan Pioneer and Historical Society, volume 12, page 659, is a letter concerning the survivors of the Chicago Massacre, written October, 1812, to Colonel Proctor by Judge Woodward, in which he says:

First, there is one officer, a lieutenant of the name of Linai

T. Helm, with whom I had the happiness of a personal acquaintance. His father is a gentleman, originally of Virginia, and of the first society of the city, who has since settled in the State of New York. He is an officer of great rank, and unblemished character. The lady of this gentleman, a young and amiable victim of misfortune, was separated from her husband. She was delivered up to her father-in-law, who was present. Mr. Helm was transported into the Indian country a hundred miles from the scene of action, and has not since been heard of at this place.

She was captured during the fight and delivered to her step-father, Mr. John Kinzie. Her own account is given in the extract from *Waubun*.

Lieutenant Helm's feeling against Captain Heald was due to the latter's refusal to take any advice from those who thoroughly understood the Indians with whom they had to deal, and his failure to consult any of his junior officers as to what course might be pursued to save the garrison.

Kirkland, in his *Story of Chicago*, chapter 8, says: "Captain Heald's conduct seems like that of a brave fool." Captain Heald was by no means a fool, but he was afraid to take any responsibility. He considered a soldier's first duty obedience to orders. If in carrying out the orders he had received from General Hull he sacrificed his command, it would not be his fault, but Hull's; whereas, if he disobeyed instructions and remained in the fort awaiting reinforcements, any disastrous results would be visited upon him alone. He was willing, however, to accept John Kinzie's offer to provide a forged order, purporting to come from General Hull, authorizing the destruction of all arms, ammunition, and liquor before evacuating the fort, instead of giving them to the savages.

Lieutenant Helm was promoted to a captaincy, but as his wound continued very troublesome he resigned from the army soon afterward, and retired to private life.

The experiences of Mrs. Helm and of her mother, Mrs. John Kinzie, were related by them personally to Mrs. Juliette A. Kinzie, the author of *Waubun*.

The little captive stolen by the Senecas and adopted into the tribe by their famous chief, "The Corn Planter," was Eleanor Lytle. She afterwards was rescued and became the wife of John Kinzie. To her daughter-in-law, Mrs. Juliette A. Kinzie, she told the story of her captivity among the Senecas, and her experiences during the Chicago Massacre.

It seems proper in giving Lieutenant Helm's account of Fort Dearborn Massacre to preface it with a letter written by Judge Augustus B. Woodward of Detroit, of which two copies exist: one of the original draft, and one of the letter sent. They differ only in some unimportant details.

Detroit was surrendered the day before the Chicago Massacre took place. As soon as information of the tragedy reached Detroit, Judge Woodward appealed to Colonel Proctor in behalf of the prisoners and possible survivors of the Massacre at Fort Dearborn.

The information given by Judge Woodward in this letter to Colonel Proctor probably came from William Griffith, a survivor who had reached Detroit. It could not have come from Lieutenant Helm, who had been sent as a prisoner to Peoria, Illinois, and did not reach St. Louis until October 14.

Nelly Kinzie Gordon.

Letters

Territory of Michigan,
October 8th, 1812.

Sir:

It is already known to you that on Saturday the fifteenth day of August last, an order having been given to evacuate Fort Dearborn an attack was made by the savages of the vicinity on the troops and persons appertaining to that garrison on their march, at the distance of about three miles from the fort, and the greater part of the number barbarously and inhumanly massacred.

Three of the survivors of that unhappy and terrible disaster having since reached this country, I have employed some pains to collect the number and names of those who were not immediately slain and to ascertain whether any hopes might yet be entertained of saving the remainder.

It is on this subject that I wish to interest your feelings and to solicit the benefit of your interposition; convinced that you estimate humanity among the brightest virtues of the soldier.

I find, sir, that the party consisted of ninety-three persons. Of these the military, including officers, non-commissioned officers and privates, amounted to fifty-four—the citizens, not acting in a military capacity, consisted of twelve. The number of women was nine, and that of the children eighteen.

The whole of the citizens were slaughtered, two women

and twelve children.

Of the military, twenty-six were killed at the time of the attack, and accounts have arrived of at least five of the surviving prisoners having been put to death in the course of the same night.

There will remain then twenty-three of the military, seven women and six children, whose fate, with the exception of the three who have come in, and of two others who are known to be in safety at St. Joseph's, remains to be yet ascertained. Of these, amounting in all to thirty-one persons, I will furnish you with the names of all that I have been able to identify.

First: there is one officer, a lieutenant, of the name of Linai T. Helm, with whom I have had the honour of a personal acquaintance. He is an officer of great merit, and of the most unblemished character. His father is a gentleman originally of Virginia, and of the first respectability, who has since settled in the State of New York. The lady of this gentleman, a young and amiable victim of misfortune, was separated from her husband during the fight. She is understood to be now at St. Joseph's. Mr. Helm was conveyed a hundred miles into the Indian country, and no accounts of his fate have yet reached this quarter.

Second: of the six non-commissioned officers, four survived the action: John Crozier, a sergeant; Daniel Dougherty, a corporal; one other corporal by the name of Bowen, and William Griffin (Griffith), sergeant, now here.

Third: of the privates it is said that five, and it is not known how many more, were put to death in the night after the action. Of those who are said to have thus suffered, I have been able to collect only the names of two; Richard Garner and James Latta. Mr. Burns, a citizen, severely wounded, was killed by an Indian woman, in the daytime, about an hour after the action. Micajah Dennison and John Fury were so badly wounded in the action that little hope was indulged of their recovery.

There will thus remain twenty to be accounted for, of

whom I can only give the following names: Dyson Dyer, William Nelson Hunt, Duncan McCarty, Augustus Mott, John Smith, John Smith, his son, a fifer, James Van Horn.

Four: of the five women whose fate remains to be ascertained, I am enabled to give the names of them all. They were Mrs. Burns, wife to the citizen before mentioned as killed after the attack; Mrs. Holt, Mrs. Lee, Mrs. Needs, and Mrs. Simmons. Among these women six children saved out of the whole number, which was eighteen; part of them belonging to the surviving mothers, and part to those who were slain.

As to the means of preserving these unhappy survivors from the distressing calamities which environ them, if they have preserved their lives, and which the rigors of the approaching season cannot fail to heighten, I would beg leave to suggest the following:

First: to send a special messenger to that quarter, overland, and with such safeguard of Indians or others, as can be procured, charged with collecting the prisoners who may yet survive, and accounts of those who may have ultimately suffered, and supplied with the means of conveying them either to Detroit or Michillimackinac.

Second: to communicate to Captain Roberts, who now commands at Michillimackinac, the circumstances of the same in full, and to request his co-operation in effecting the humane object of their ultimate preservation.

I am not authorized by my government to make the assurance, but I shall not doubt their cheerfully defraying such expense of ransom, or conveyance, as circumstances will justify; and private funds are also ready to be applied to the same purpose. I do not less doubt your willing and zealous assistance, and with a confident hope of it, permit me, sir, to assure you of the high respect with which I have the honour to be

     Your obedient servant,

       A. B. Woodward.

To Col. Henry Proctor.

Flemington, New Jersey,
6th June, 1814.

Dear Sir:—

I hope you will excuse the length of time I have taken to communicate the history of the unfortunate massacre of Chicago. It is now nearly finished, and in two weeks you may expect it. As the history cannot possibly be written with truth without eternally disgracing Major Heald, I wish you could find out whether I shall be cashiered or censured for bringing to light the conduct of so great a man as many think him. You know I am the only officer that has escaped to tell the news. Some of the men have got off, but where they are I know not; they would be able to testify to some of the principal facts. I have waited a long time expecting a court of inquiry on his conduct but see plainly it is to be overlooked. I am resolved now to do myself justice even if I have to leave the service to publish the history. I shall be happy to hear from you immediately on the receipt of this.

I have the honour to be sir,
with great respect,
Your obedient servant,
L. T. Helm.

Augustus B. Woodward, Esqr.
Washington City

(Addressed:)   Flemington, Jan. 6th.
Augustus B. Woodward, Esq.
Milton, Va.

(Endorsed:)   Helm, Mr. Linah T.
letter from
Dated Flemington,
New Jersey, June 6th, 1814.
Received at Washington.
June 14th, 1814.

R. June 14th, 1814.

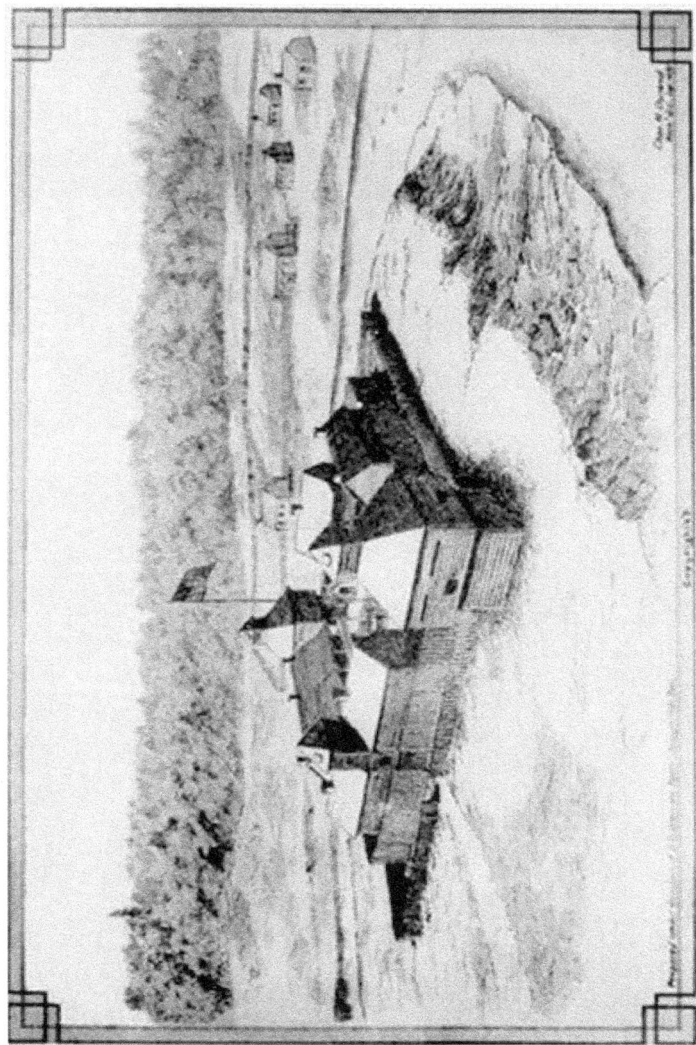

Old Fort Dearborn

Lieutenant Helm's Narrative

Sometime in April, about the 7th-10, a party of Winnebagoes came to Chicago and murdered two men. This gave sufficient ground to suppose the Indians hostile, as they have left every sign by scalping them and leaving a weapon, say a war mallet, as a token of their returning in June. Mr. Kinzie sent a letter from the Interior of the Indian Country to inform Captain Heald that the Indians were hostile inclined and only waiting the Declaration of War to commence open hostilities. This they told Kinzie in confidence on the 10th of July. Captain Heald got the information of War being declared, and on the 8th of August got General Hull's order to evacuate the Post of Fort Dearborn by the route of Detroit, or Fort Wayne, if practicable.

This letter was brought by a Potowautemie Chief Winnemeg, and he informed Captain Heald, through Kenzie, to evacuate immediately the next day, if possible, as the Indians were hostile and that the troops should change the usual routes to go to Fort Wayne. On the 12th August, Captain William Wells arrived from Fort Wayne with 27 Miamis, and after a council being held by him with the tribes there assembled to amount of 500 warriors 179 women and children. He after council declared them hostile and that his opinion was that they would interrupt us on our route.

Captain Wells enquired into the State of the arms, ammunition and provisions. We had 200 stand of arms, four pieces of artillery, 6,000 lbs. of powder and a sufficient quantity of shot lead, etc. three months provisions taken in Indian corn and all

23

this on the 12th of August, having prior to this expended three months provisions at least in the interval between the 7th and 12th of August, exclusive of this we had at our command 200 head of horned cattle and 27 barrels of salt. After this survey, Wells demanded of Captain Heald if he intended to evacuate. His answer was he would. Kenzie then, with Lieutenant Helm, called on Wells and requested him to call on Captain Heald and cause the ammunition and arms to be destroyed, but Captain Wells insisted on Kenzie and Helm to join with him.

This being done, Captain Heald hesitated and observed that it was not sound policy to tell a lie to an Indian; that he had received a positive order from General Hull to deliver up to those Indians all the public property of whatsoever nature particularly to those Indians that would take in the Troops and that he could not alter it, and that it might irritate the Indians and be the means of the destruction of his men. Kenzie volunteered to take the responsibility on himself, provided Captain Heald would consider the method he would point out a safe one, he agreed. Kenzie wrote an order as if from General Hull, and gave it into Captain Heald.

It was supposed to answer and accordingly was carried into effect. The ammunition and muskets were all destroyed the night of the 13th. The 15th, we evacuated the garrison, and about one and half mile from the garrison we were informed by Captain Wells that we were surrounded and the attack by the Indians began about 10 of the clock morning. The men in a few minutes were, with the exception of ten, all killed and wounded. The ensign and surgeons mate were both killed. The captain and myself both badly wounded during the battle. I fired my piece at an Indian and felt confident I killed him or wounded him badly. I immediately called to the men to follow me in the pirara, or we would be shot down before we could load our guns.

We had proceeded under a heavy fire about an hundred and five paces when I made a wheel to the left to observe the motion of the Indians and avoid being shot in the back, which I had so far miraculously escaped. Just as I wheeled I received a ball through my coat pocket, which struck the barrel of my gun and fell in the lining of my coat. In a few seconds, I received a ball in my right foot, which lamed me considerably. The Indians happened immediately to stop firing and never more renewed it. I immediately ordered the men that were able to load their guns and commenced loading for them that were not able. I now discovered Captain Heald for the first time to my knowledge during the battle. He was coming from towards the Indians and to my great surprise they never offered to fire on him.

He came up and ordered the men to form; that his intentions were to charge the body of Indians that were on the bank of the lake where we had just retreated from. They appeared to be about 300 strong. We were 27, including all the wounded. He advanced about 5 steps and not at all to my surprise was the first that halted. Some of the men fell back instead of advancing. We then gained the only high piece of ground there was near. We now had a little time to reflect and saw death in every direction.

At this time an interpreter from the Indians advanced towards us and called for the captain, who immediately went to meet him (the interpreter was a half Indian and had lived a long time within a few yards of the fort and bound to Mr. Kinzie; he was always very friendly with us all). A chief by the name of Blackbird advanced to the interpreter and met the captain, who after a few words conversation delivered him his sword, and in a few minutes returned to us and informed me he had offered 100 dollars for every man that was then living. He said they were then deciding on what to do.

They, however, in a few minutes, called him again and talked with him some time, when he returned and informed me they had agreed if I and the men would surrender by laying down our arms they would lay down theirs, meet us half way, shake us by the hand as friends and take us back to the fort. I asked him if he knew what they intended doing with us then. He said they did not inform him. He asked me if I would surrender. The men were at this time crowding to my back and began to beg me not to surrender. I told them not to be uneasy for I had already done my best for them and was determined not to surrender unless I saw better prospects of us all being saved and then not without they were willing.

The captain asked me the second time what I would do, without an answer. I discovered the interpreter at this time running from the Indians towards us, and when he came in about twenty steps the captain put the question the third time. The interpreter called out, "Lieutenant don't surrender for if you do they will kill you all, for there has been no general council held with them yet. You must wait, and I will go back and hold a general council with them and return and let you know what they will do." I told him to go, for I had no idea of surrender.

He went and collected all the Indians and talked for some time, when he returned and told me the Indians said if I would surrender as before described they would not kill any, and said it was his opinion they would do as they said, for they had already saved Mr. Kinzie and some of the women and children. This enlivened me and the men, for we well knew Mr. Kinzie stood higher than any man in that country among the Indians, and he might be the means of saving us from utter destruction, which afterwards proved to be the case. We then surrendered, and after the Indians had fired off our guns they put the captain and myself and some of the wounded men on horses and marched us to the bank of the lake, where the battle first commenced.

When we arrived at the bank and looked down on the sand beach I was struck with horror at the sight of men, women and children lying naked with principally all their heads off, and in passing over the bodies I was confident I saw my wife with her head off about two feet from her shoulders. Tears for the first time rushed in my eyes, but I consoled myself with a firm belief that I should soon follow her. I now began to repent that I had ever surrendered, but it was too late to recall, and we had only to look up to Him who had first caused our existence.

When we had arrived in half a mile of the fort they halted us, made the men sit down, form a ring around them, began to take off their hats and strip the captain. They attempted to strip me, but were prevented by a chief who stuck close to me. I made signs to him that I wanted to drink, for the weather was very warm. He led me off towards the fort and, to my great astonishment, saw my wife sitting among some squaws crying.

Our feelings can be better judged than expressed. They brought some water and directed her to wash and dress my wound, which she did, and bound it up with her pocket handkerchief. They then brought up some of the men and tommyhawked one of them before us. They now took Mrs. Helm across the river (for we were nearly on its banks) to Mr. Kinzie's. We met again at my father's in the State of New York, she having arrived seven days before me after being separated seven months and one week. She was taken in the direction of Detroit and I was taken down to Illinois River and was sold to Mr. Thomas Forsyth, half brother of Mr. Kinzie's, who, a short time after, effected my escape. This gentleman was the means of saving many lives on the warring (?) frontier. I was taken on the 15th of August and arrived safe among the Americans at St. Louis on the 14th of October.

Captain Heald, through Kenzie, sending his two negroes, got put on board an Indian boat going to St. Joseph, and from that place got to Makenac by Lake Michigan in a birch canoe.

The night of the 14th, the interpreter and a chief (Black Partridge) waited on Captain Heald. The Indian gave up his medal and told Heald to beware of the next day, that the Indians would destroy him and his men. This Heald never communicated to one of his officers. There was but Captain Wells that was acquainted with it. You will observe, sir, that I did, with Kenzie, protest against destroying the arms, ammunition and provisions until that Heald told me positively that he would evacuate at all hazards.

15th of August, we evacuated the fort. The number of soldiers was 52 privates and musicians (2), 4 officers and physicians, 14 citizens, 18 children and 9 women, the baggage being in front with the citizens, women and children and on the margin of the lake, we having advanced to gain the prairie. I could not see the massacre, but Kinzie, with Doctor Van Vorees, being ordered by Captain Heald to take charge of the women and children, remained on the beach, and Kinzie since told me he was an eye witness to the horrid scene. The Indians came down on the baggage wagons for plunder. They butchered every male citizen but Kinzie, two women and 12 children in the most inhuman manner possible, opened them, cutting off their heads and taken out their hearts; several of the women were wounded but not dangerously.

LIST OF GARRISON

Nathan Heald	1	Released.
Lina T. Helm	2	Released
Nathan Edson	3	——
Elias Mills	4	——
Thos. Point Dexter	5	——
August Mort	6	Died natural.
James Latta	7	Killed.
Michael Lynch	8	Killed.
John Sullinfield	9	Killed.
John Smith, Senr.	10	Released.
John Smith, Junr.	11	——
Nathan Hunt	12	Deserted.
Richard Garner	13	Killed.
Paul Greene	14	——
James V—tworth (?)	15	——
John Griffiths	16	Supposed to be a Frenchman and released.
Joseph Bowen	17	Supposed to be a Frenchman and released.
John Ferry (or Fury)	18	——
John Crozier	19	Deserted.
John Needs	20	——
Daniel Daugherty	21	——
Dyson Dyer	22	Killed.

John Andrews	23 Killed.
James Stone (or Starr or Storr)	24 Killed.
Joseph Nolis (or Notts)	25 ——
James Corbin	26 ——
Fielding Corbin	27 ——

Citizens:

Jos. Burns   28 Mortally wounded since
                                        killed.

(Names of women on reverse page)
Women taken prisoners:

Mrs. Heald	Released.
Mrs. Helm	Released
Mrs. Holt	Prisoners
Mrs. Burns	Prisoners
Mrs. Leigh	Prisoners
Mrs. Simmons	Prisoners
Mrs. Needs	Prisoners

Killed in action:

Mrs. Corbin.
Mrs. Heald's Negro woman.

Children yet in captivity:

Mrs. Leigh's 2, one since dead N D.
Mrs. Burns' 2.
Mrs. Simmons' 1.
13 children killed during the action.
11 citizens including Captain Wells.
John Kinzie taken, but not considered as a prisoner of war.
54 Rank and file left the garrison.

The Massacre at Chicago

(This narrative related by two of the survivors, Mrs. John Kinzie and Mrs. Helm, to Mrs. Juliette A. Kinzie, is taken from *Waubun*. It was first published in pamphlet form in 1836; was transferred, with little variation, to Brown's *History of Illinois*, and to a work called *Western Annals*. Major Richardson likewise made it the basis of his two tales, *Hardscrabble*, and *Wau-nan-gee*.)

It was the evening of April 7, 1812. The children were dancing before the fire to the music of their father's violin. The tea table was spread, and they were awaiting the return of their mother, who had gone to visit a sick neighbour about a quarter of a mile up the river.

Suddenly their sports were interrupted. The door was thrown open, and Mrs. Kinzie rushed in, pale with terror, and scarcely able to speak. "The Indians! the Indians!" she gasped.

"The Indians? What? Where?" they all demanded in alarm.

"Up at Lee's Place, killing and scalping!"

With difficulty Mrs. Kinzie composed herself sufficiently to say that, while she was at Burns', a man and a boy had been seen running down with all speed on the opposite side of the river. They had called across to the Burns family to save themselves, for the Indians were at Lee's Place, from which the two had just made their escape. Having given this terrifying news, they had made all speed for the fort, which was on the same side of the river.

All was now consternation and dismay in the Kinzie household. The family were hurried into two old pirogues that lay moored near the house, and paddled with all possible haste across the river to take refuge in the fort.

All that the man and boy who had made their escape were able to tell was soon known; but, in order to render their story more intelligible, it is necessary to describe the situation.

Lee's Place, since known as Hardscrabble, was a farm intersected by the Chicago River, about four miles from its mouth. The farmhouse stood on the west bank of the south branch of this river. On the north side of the main stream, but near its junction with Lake Michigan, stood the dwelling house and trading establishment of Mr. Kinzie.

The fort was situated on the southern bank, directly opposite this mansion, the river and a few rods of sloping green turf on either side being all that intervened between them.

The fort was differently constructed from the one erected on the same site in 1816. It had two blockhouses on the southern side, and on the northern a sally port, or subterranean passage from the parade ground to the river. This was designed to facilitate escape in case of an emergency or as a means of supplying the garrison with water during a siege.

In the fort at this period were three officers, Captain Heald, who was in command, Lieutenant Helm, the son-in-law of Mr. Kinzie, and Ensign Ronan—the last two very young men—and the surgeon, Dr. Van Voorhees.

The garrison numbered about seventy-five men, very few of whom were effective.

A constant and friendly intercourse had been maintained between these troops and the Indians. It is true that the principal men of the Potowatomi nation, like those of most other tribes, went yearly to Fort Malden, in Canada, to receive the large number of presents with which the British Government, for many years, had been in the habit of purchasing their alliance; and it was well known that many of the Potowatomi, as well as Winnebago, had been engaged with the Ottawa and Shawnee at the battle of Tippecanoe, the preceding autumn; yet, as the principal chiefs of all the bands in the neighbourhood appeared to be on the most amicable terms with the Americans, no interruption of their harmony was at any time anticipated.

After August 15, however, many circumstances were recalled that might have opened the eyes of the whites had they not been blinded by a false security. One incident in particular may be mentioned.

In the spring preceding the destruction of the fort, two Indians of the Calumet band came to the fort on a visit to the commanding officer. As they passed through the quarters, they saw Mrs. Heald and Mrs. Helm playing at battledoor.

Turning to the interpreter, one of them, Nau-non-gee, remarked, "The white chiefs' wives are amusing themselves very much; it will not be long before they are hoeing in our cornfields!"

At the time this was considered an idle threat, or, at most, an ebullition of jealous feeling at the contrast between the situation of their own women and that of the "white chiefs' wives." Some months after, how bitterly was it remembered!

The farm at Lee's Place was occupied by a Mr. White and three persons employed by him.

In the afternoon of the day on which our narrative commences, a party of ten or twelve Indians, dressed and painted, arrived at the house. According to the custom among savages, they entered and seated themselves without ceremony.

Something in their appearance and manner excited the suspicion of one of the household, a Frenchman, who remarked, "I do not like the looks of these Indians—they are none of our folks. I know by their dress and paint that they are not Potowatomi."

Another of the men, a discharged soldier, then said to a boy who was present, "If that is the case, we'd better get away from them if we can. Say nothing; but do as you see me do."

There were two canoes tied near the bank, and the soldier walked leisurely towards them. Some of the Indians inquired where he was going. He pointed to the cattle standing among the haystacks on the opposite bank, making signs that they must go and fodder them, and that they would then return and get their supper.

As the afternoon was far advanced, this explanation was accepted without question.

The soldier got into one canoe, and the boy into the other. The stream was narrow, and they were soon across. Having gained the opposite side, they pulled some hay for the cattle, made a show of herding them, and when they had gradually made a circuit, so that their movements were concealed by the haystacks, took to the woods, close at hand, and then started for the fort.

They had run about a quarter of a mile when they heard two guns discharged in succession. These guns they supposed to have been levelled at the companions they had left.

They ran without stopping until they arrived opposite Burns',[1] where, as before related, they called across to warn the family of their danger, and then hastened on to the fort.

It now occurred to those who had secured their own safety that the Burns family was still exposed to imminent peril. The question was, who would hazard his life to bring them to a place of security? The gallant young officer, Ensign Ronan, with a party of five or six soldiers, volunteered to go to their rescue.

They ascended the river in a scow, took the mother, with her infant, scarcely a day old, upon her bed to the boat, and carefully conveyed her with the other members of the family to the fort.

The same afternoon a party of soldiers, consisting of a corporal and six men, had obtained leave to go fishing up the river. They had not returned when the fugitives from Lee's Place arrived at the fort. It was now night and, fearing they might encounter the Indians, the commanding officer ordered a cannon fired, warning them of their danger.

It will be remembered that the unsettled state of the country after the Battle of Tippecanoe, the preceding November, had

---

1. Burns' house stood near the spot where the Agency Building, or "Cobweb Castle," was afterwards erected, at the foot of North State Street.

rendered every man vigilant, and the slightest alarm was an admonition to "beware of the Indians."

At the time the cannon was fired the fishing party were about two miles above Lee's Place. Hearing the signal, they put out their torches and dropped down the river towards the garrison, as silently as possible.

When they reached Lee's Place, it was proposed to stop and warn the inmates to be on their guard, as the signal from the fort indicated some kind of danger. All was still as death around the house. The soldiers groped their way along, and as the corporal jumped over the small inclosure he placed his hand upon the dead body of a man. He soon ascertained that the head was without a scalp, and otherwise mutilated. The faithful dog of the murdered man stood guarding the lifeless remains of his master.

The tale was told. The men retreated to their canoes, and reached the fort unmolested about eleven o'clock at night.

The next morning a party of citizens and soldiers volunteered to go to Lee's Place to learn further the fate of its occupants. The body of Mr. White was found pierced by two balls, with eleven stabs in the breast. The Frenchman also lay dead, his dog still beside him. The bodies were brought to the fort and buried in its immediate vicinity.

Later it was learned from traders out in the Indian country that the perpetrators of the deed were a party of Winnebago who had come into the neighbourhood to "take some white scalps." Their plan had been to proceed down the river from Lee's Place and kill every white man outside the walls of the fort. However, hearing the report of the cannon, and not knowing what it portended, they thought it best to retreat to their homes on Rock River.

The settlers outside the fort, a few discharged soldiers and some families of half-breeds, now intrenched themselves in the Agency House. This building stood west of the fort, between the pickets and the river, and distant about twenty rods from the former.

It was an old-fashioned log house, with a hall running through the centre, and one large room on each side. Piazzas extended the whole length of the building, in front and rear. These were now planked up, for greater security; portholes were cut, and sentinels posted at night.

As the enemy were believed to be still lurking in the neighbourhood, or, emboldened by former success, were likely to return at any moment, an order was issued prohibiting any soldier or citizen from leaving the vicinity of the garrison without a guard.

One night a sergeant and a private, who were out on patrol, came suddenly upon a party of Indians in the pasture adjoining the esplanade. The sergeant fired his piece, and both retreated towards the fort. Before they could reach it, an Indian threw his tomahawk, which missed the sergeant and struck a wagon standing near. The sentinel from the blockhouse immediately fired while the men got safely in. The next morning traces of blood were found for a considerable distance into the prairie, and from this and the appearance of the long grass, where it was evident a body had lain, it was certain some execution had been done.

On another occasion Indians entered the esplanade to steal horses. Not finding any in the stable, as they had expected to, they relieved their disappointment by stabbing all the sheep in the stable and then letting them loose. The poor animals flocked towards the fort. This gave the alarm. The garrison was aroused, and parties were sent out; but the marauders escaped unmolested. The inmates of the fort experienced no further alarm for many weeks.

On the afternoon of August 7, Winnemeg, or Catfish, a Potowatomi chief, arrived at the post, bringing dispatches from General Hull. These announced that war had been declared between the United States and Great Britain, and that General Hull, at the head of the Northwestern army, had arrived at Detroit; also, that the Island of Mackinac had fallen into the hands of the British.

The orders to Captain Heald were to "evacuate the fort, if

practicable, and, in that event, to distribute all the United States property contained in the fort, and in the United States factory or agency, among the Indians in the neighbourhood."

After having delivered his dispatches, Winnemeg requested a private interview with Mr. Kinzie, who had taken up his residence in the fort. He told Mr. Kinzie he was acquainted with the purport of the communications he had brought, and begged him to ascertain if it were the intention of Captain Heald to evacuate the post. He advised strongly against such a step, inasmuch as the garrison was well supplied with ammunition, and with provisions for six months. It would, therefore, be far better, he thought, to remain until reinforcements could be sent. If, however, Captain Heald should decide to leave the post, it should by all means be done immediately. The Potowatomi, through whose country they must pass, being ignorant of the object of Winnemeg's mission, a forced march might be made before the hostile Indians were prepared to interrupt them.

Of this advice, so earnestly given, Captain Heald was immediately informed. He replied that it was his intention to evacuate the post, but that, inasmuch as he had received orders to distribute the United States property, he should not feel justified in leaving until he had collected the Indians of the neighbourhood and made an equitable division among them.

Winnemeg then suggested the expediency of marching out, and leaving all things standing; possibly while the Indians were engaged in the partition of the spoils the troops might effect their retreat unmolested. This advice, strongly seconded by Mr. Kinzie, did not meet the approbation of the commanding officer.

The order to evacuate the post was read next morning upon parade. It is difficult to understand why, in such an emergency, Captain Heald omitted the usual form of holding a council of war with his officers. It can be accounted for only by the fact of a want of harmonious feeling between him and one of his junior officers, Ensign Ronan, a high-spirited and somewhat overbearing, but brave and generous, young man.

In the course of the day, no council having been called, the officers waited on Captain Heald, seeking information regarding the course he intended to pursue. When they learned his intentions, they remonstrated with him, on the following grounds:

First, it was highly improbable that the command would be permitted to pass through the country in safety to Fort Wayne. For although it had been said that some of the chiefs had opposed an attack upon the fort, planned the preceding autumn, yet it was well known that they had been actuated in that matter by motives of personal regard for one family, that of Mr. Kinzie, and not by any general friendly feeling towards the Americans; and that, in any event, it was hardly to be expected that these few individuals would be able to control the whole tribe, who were thirsting for blood.

In the next place, their march must necessarily be slow, as their movements must be accommodated to the helplessness of the women and children, of whom there were a number with the detachment. Of their small force some of the soldiers were superannuated, others invalid.

Therefore, since the course to be pursued was left discretional, their unanimous advice was to remain where they were, and fortify themselves as strongly as possible. Succour from the other side of the peninsula might arrive before they could be attacked by the British from Mackinac; and even should help not come, it were far better to fall into the hands of the British than to become the victims of the savages.

Captain Heald argued in reply that "a special order had been issued by the War Department that no post should be surrendered without battle having been given, and his force was totally inadequate to an engagement with the Indians; that he should unquestionably be censured for remaining when there appeared a prospect of a safe march through; and that, upon the whole, he deemed it expedient to assemble the Indians, distribute the property among them, and then ask them for an escort to Fort Wayne, with the promise of a considerable reward upon their safe arrival, adding that he had full confidence in the friendly professions of the Indians, from whom, as well as from the soldiers, the capture of Mackinac had been kept a profound secret."

From this time the officers held themselves aloof, and spoke but little upon the subject, though they considered Captain Heald's project little short of madness. The dissatisfaction among the soldiers increased hourly, until it reached a high pitch of insubordination.

On one occasion, when conversing with Mr. Kinzie upon the parade, Captain Heald remarked, "I could not remain, even if I thought it best, for I have but a small store of provisions."

"Why, captain," said a soldier who stood near, forgetting all etiquette in the excitement of the moment, "you have cattle enough to last the troops six months."

"But," replied Captain Heald, "I have no salt to preserve it with."

"Then jerk it," said the man, "as the Indians do their venison."

The Indians now became daily more unruly. Entering the fort in defiance of the sentinels, they made their way without ceremony into the officers' quarters. One day an Indian took up a rifle and fired it in the parlour of the commanding officer, as an expression of defiance. Some believed that this was intended among the young men as a signal for an attack. The old chiefs passed backwards and forwards among the assembled groups with the appearance of the most lively agitation, while the squaws rushed to and fro in great excitement, evidently prepared for some fearful scene.

Any further manifestation of ill feeling was, however, suppressed for the time and, strange as it may seem, Captain Heald continued to entertain a conviction of having created so amicable a disposition among the Indians as to insure the safety of the command on their march to Fort Wayne.

Thus passed the time until August 12. The feelings of the inmates of the fort during this time may be better imagined than described. Each morning that dawned seemed to bring them nearer to that most appalling fate—butchery by a savage foe; and at night they scarcely dared yield to slumber, lest they should be aroused by the war whoop and tomahawk. Gloom and mistrust prevailed, and the want of unanimity among the officers prevented the consolation they might have found in mutual sympathy and encouragement.

The Indians being assembled from the neighbouring villages, a council was held with them on the afternoon of August 12. Captain Heald alone attended on the part of the military. He had requested his officers to accompany him, but they had declined. They had been secretly informed that the young chiefs intended to fall upon the officers and massacre them while in council, but they could not persuade Captain Heald of the truth of their information. They waited therefore only until, accompanied by Mr. Kinzie, he had left the garrison, when they took command of the blockhouses overlooking the esplanade on which the council was held, opened the portholes, and pointed the cannon so as to command the whole assembly. By this means, probably, the lives of the whites who were present in council were preserved.

In council, the commanding officer informed the Indians that it was his intention to distribute among them, the next day, not only the goods lodged in the United States factory, but also the ammunition and provisions, with which the garrison was well supplied. He then requested the Potowatomi to furnish him an escort to Fort Wayne, promising them, in addition to the presents they were now about to receive, a liberal reward on arriving there. With many professions of friendship and good will, the savages assented to all he proposed, and promised all he required.

After the council, Mr. Kinzie, who well understood not only the Indian character but the present tone of feeling among them, had a long interview with Captain Heald, in hopes of opening his eyes to the real state of affairs.

He reminded him that since the trouble with the Indians along the Wabash and in the vicinity, there had appeared to be a settled plan of hostilities towards the whites, in consequence of which it had been the policy of the Americans to withhold from the Indians whatever would enable them to carry on their warfare upon the defenceless inhabitants of the frontier.

Mr. Kinzie also recalled to Captain Heald how, having left home for Detroit, the preceding autumn, on receiving news at De Charme's[2] of the Battle of Tippecanoe, he had immediately returned to Chicago, that he might dispatch orders to his traders to furnish no ammunition to the Indians. As a result, all the ammunition the traders had on hand was secreted, and those traders who had not already started for their wintering grounds took neither powder nor shot with them.

Captain Heald was struck with the inadvisability of furnishing the enemy (for such they must now consider their old neighbours) with arms against himself, and determined to destroy all the ammunition except what should be necessary for the use of his own troops.

On August 13 the goods, consisting of blankets, broadcloths, calicoes, paints, and miscellaneous supplies were distributed, as stipulated. The same evening part of the ammunition and liquor was carried into the sally port, and there thrown into a well which had been dug to supply the garrison with water in case of emergency. The remainder was transported, as secretly as possible, through the northern gate; the heads of the barrels were knocked in, and the contents poured into the river.

The same fate was shared by a large quantity of alcohol belonging to Mr. Kinzie, which had been deposited in a warehouse near his residence opposite the fort.

The Indians suspected what was going on, and crept, serpent-like, as near the scene of action as possible; but a vigilant watch was kept up, and no one was suffered to approach but those engaged in the affair. All the muskets not necessary for the command on the march were broken up and thrown into the well, together with bags of shot, flints, gunscrews; in short, everything relating to weapons of defense.

Some relief to the general feeling of despondency was af-

2. A trading-establishment—now, (as at time of first publication), Ypsilanti.

forded by the arrival, on August 14, of Captain Wells[3] with fifteen friendly Miami.

Of this brave man, who forms so conspicuous a figure in our frontier annals, it is unnecessary here to say more than that he had resided from boyhood among the Indians, and hence possessed a perfect knowledge of their character and habits.

At Fort Wayne he had heard of the order to evacuate the fort at Chicago, and, knowing the hostile determination of the Potowatomi, had made a rapid march across the country to prevent the exposure of his relative, Captain Heald, and his troops to certain destruction.

But he came "all too late." When he reached the post he found that the ammunition had been destroyed, and the provisions given to the Indians. There was, therefore, no alternative, and every preparation was made for the march of the troops on the following morning.

On the afternoon of the same day a second council was held with the Indians. They expressed great indignation at the destruction of the ammunition and liquor. Notwithstanding the precautions that had been taken to preserve secrecy, the noise of knocking in the heads of the barrels had betrayed the operations of the preceding night; indeed, so great was the quantity of liquor thrown into the river that next morning the water was, as one expressed it, "strong grog."

Murmurs and threats were everywhere heard among the savages. It was evident that the first moment of exposure would subject the troops to some manifestation of their disappointment and resentment.

Among the chiefs were several who, although they shared the general hostile feeling of their tribe towards the Americans, yet retained a personal regard for the troops at this post and for the few white citizens of the place. These chiefs exerted their utmost influence to allay the revengeful feelings of the young men, and

3. Captain Wells, when a boy, was stolen by the Miami Indians from the family of Hon. Nathaniel Pope in Kentucky. Although recovered by them, he preferred to return and live among his new friends. He married a Miami woman, and became a chief of the nation. He was the father of Mrs. Judge Wolcott of Maumee, Ohio.

to avert their sanguinary designs, but without effect.

On the evening succeeding the council Black Partridge, a conspicuous chief, entered the quarters of the commanding officer.

"Father," said he, "I come to deliver up to you the medal I wear. It was given me by the Americans, and I have long worn it in token of our mutual friendship. But our young men are resolved to imbrue their hands in the blood of the whites. I cannot restrain them, and I will not wear a token of peace while I am compelled to act as an enemy."

Had further evidence been wanting, this circumstance would have sufficiently justified the devoted band in their melancholy anticipations. Nevertheless, they went steadily on with the necessary preparations; and, amid the horrors of the situation there were not wanting gallant hearts who strove to encourage in their desponding companions the hopes of escape they themselves were far from indulging.

Of the ammunition there had been reserved but twenty-five rounds, besides one box of cartridges, contained in the baggage wagons. This must, under any circumstances of danger, have proved an inadequate supply; but the prospect of a fatiguing march, in their present ineffective state, forbade the troops embarrassing themselves with a larger quantity.

The morning of August 15 arrived. Nine o'clock was the hour named for starting and all things were in readiness.

Mr. Kinzie, having volunteered to accompany the troops in their march, had intrusted his family to the care of some friendly Indians, who promised to convey them in a boat around the head of Lake Michigan to a point[4] on the St. Joseph River, there to be joined by the troops, should their march be permitted.

Early in the morning Mr. Kinzie received a message from To-pee-nee-bee, a chief of the St. Joseph band, informing him that mischief was intended by the Potowatomi who had engaged to escort the detachment, and urging him to relinquish his plan of

---

4. The spot now called Bertrand, then known as *Parc aux Vaches*, from its having been a favourite "stamping-ground" of the buffalo which abounded in the country.

accompanying the troops by land, promising him that the boat containing his family should be permitted to pass in safety to St. Joseph.

Mr. Kinzie declined this proposal, as he believed his presence might restrain the fury of the savages, so warmly were the greater number of them attached to him and his family.

Seldom does one find a man who, like John Kinzie, refuses safety for himself in order to stand or fall with his countrymen, and who, as stern as any Spartan, bids farewell to his dear ones to go forward to almost certain destruction.

The party in the boat consisted of Mrs. Kinzie and her four younger children, their nurse Josette, a clerk of Mr. Kinzie's, two servants, and the boatmen, besides the two Indians who were to act as their protectors. The boat started, but had scarcely reached the mouth of the river, which, it will be recalled, was here half a mile below the fort, when another messenger from To-pee-nee-bee arrived to detain it. There was no mistaking the meaning of this detention.

In breathless anxiety sat the wife and mother. She was a woman of unusual energy and strength of character, yet her heart died within her as she folded her arms about her helpless infants and gazed upon the march of her husband and eldest child to what seemed certain death.

As the troops left the fort, the band struck up the Dead March. On they came, in military array, but with solemn mien, Captain Wells in the lead at the head of his little band of Miami. He had blackened his face before leaving the garrison, in token of his impending fate. The troops took their route along the lake shore; but when they reached the point where the range of sand hills intervening between the prairie and the beach commenced, the escort of Potowatomi, in number about five hundred, took the level of the prairie, instead of continuing along the shore with the Americans and Miami.

They had marched perhaps a mile and a half when Captain Wells, who had kept somewhat in advance with his Miami, came riding furiously back.

"They are about to attack us," shouted he; "form instantly, and charge upon them."

Scarcely were the words uttered, when a volley was showered from among the sand hills. The troops, brought hastily into line, charged up the bank. One man, a veteran of seventy winters, fell as they ascended. The remainder of the scene is best described in the words of an eyewitness and participator in the tragedy, Mrs. Helm,[5] the wife of Captain (then Lieutenant) Helm, and stepdaughter of Mr. Kinzie.

> After we had left the bank the firing became general. The Miami fled at the outset. Their chief rode up to the Potowatomi, and said: 'You have deceived us and the Americans. You have done a bad action, and (brandishing his tomahawk) I will be the first to head a party of Americans to return and punish your treachery.' So saying, he galloped after his companions, who were now scurrying across the prairies.
>
> The troops behaved most gallantly. They were but a handful, but they seemed resolved to sell their lives as dearly as possible. Our horses pranced and bounded, and could hardly be restrained as the balls whistled among them. I drew off a little, and gazed upon my husband and father, who were yet unharmed. I felt that my hour was come, and endeavoured to forget those I loved, and prepare myself for my approaching fate.
>
> While I was thus engaged, the surgeon, Dr. Van Voorhees, came up. He was badly wounded. His horse had been shot under him, and he had received a ball in his leg. Every muscle of his face was quivering with the agony of terror. He said to me, 'Do you think they will take our lives? I am badly wounded, but I think not mortally. Perhaps we might purchase our lives by promising them a large reward. Do you think there is any chance?'

---

5. Mrs. Helm is represented by the female figure in the bronze group erected by George M. Pullman, at the foot of 18th Street, to commemorate the massacre which took place at that spot.

'Dr. Van Voorhees,' said I, 'do not let us waste the moments that yet remain to us in such vain hopes. Our fate is inevitable. In a few moments we must appear before the bar of God. Let us make what preparation is yet in our power.'

'Oh, I cannot die!' exclaimed he, 'I am not fit to die—if I had but a short time to prepare—death is awful!'

I pointed to Ensign Ronan, who, though mortally wounded and nearly down, was still fighting with desperation on one knee.[6]

'Look at that man!' said I. 'At least he dies like a soldier.'

'Yes,' replied the unfortunate surgeon, with a convulsive gasp, 'but he has no terrors of the future—he is an atheist.'

At this moment a young Indian raised his tomahawk over me. Springing aside, I partially avoided the blow, which, intended for my skull, fell on my shoulder. I seized the Indian around the neck, and while exerting my utmost strength to get possession of his scalping-knife, hanging in a scabbard over his breast, I was dragged from his grasp by another and older Indian.

The latter bore me struggling and resisting towards the lake. Despite the rapidity with which I was hurried along, I recognized, as I passed, the lifeless remains of the unfortunate surgeon. Some murderous tomahawk had stretched him upon the very spot where I had last seen him.

I was immediately plunged into the water and held there with a forcible hand, notwithstanding my resistance. I soon perceived, however, that the object of my captor was not to drown me, for he held me firmly in such a position as to keep my head above water. This reassured me, and, regarding him attentively, I soon recognized, in spite of the paint with which he was disguised, the Black Partridge.

"When the firing had nearly subsided, my preserver bore me from the water and conducted me up the sand banks.

---

6. The exact spot of this encounter was about where 21st Street crosses Indiana Avenue.

It was a burning August morning, and walking through the sand in my drenched condition was inexpressibly painful and fatiguing. I stooped and took off my shoes to free them from the sand with which they were nearly filled, when a squaw seized and carried them off, and I was obliged to proceed without them.

When we had gained the prairie, I was met by my father, who told me that my husband was safe and but slightly wounded. I was led gently back towards the Chicago River, along the southern bank of which was the Potowatomi encampment. Once I was placed upon a horse without a saddle, but, finding the motion insupportable, I sprang off. Assisted partly by my kind conductor, Black Partridge, and partly by another Indian, Pee-so-tum, who held dangling in his hand a scalp which by the black ribbon around the queue I recognized as that of Captain Wells, I dragged my fainting steps to one of the *wigwams*.

The wife of Wau-bee-nee-mah, a chief from the Illinois River, was standing near. Seeing my exhausted condition, she seized a kettle, dipped up some water from a stream that flowed near,[7] threw into it some maple sugar, and, stirring it with her hand, gave it to me to drink. This act of kindness, in the midst of so many horrors, touched me deeply. But my attention was soon diverted to other things.

The fort, since the troops marched out, had become a scene of plunder. The cattle had been shot as they ran at large, and lay about, dead or dying. This work of butchery had commenced just as we were leaving the fort. I vividly recalled a remark of Ensign Ronan, as the firing went on. 'Such,' turning to me, 'is to be our fate—to be shot down like brutes!'

'Well, sir,' said the commanding officer, who overheard him, 'are you afraid?'

'No,' replied the high-spirited young man, 'I can march

---

7. Along the present State Street.

up to the enemy where you dare not show your face.' And his subsequent gallant behaviour showed this was no idle boast.

As the noise of the firing grew gradually fainter and the stragglers from the victorious party came dropping in, I received confirmation of what my father had hurriedly communicated in our meeting on the lake shore: the whites had surrendered, after the loss of about two thirds of their number. They had stipulated, through the interpreter, Peresh Leclerc, that their lives and those of the remaining women and children be spared, and that they be delivered in safety at certain of the British posts, unless ransomed by traders in the Indian country. It appears that the wounded prisoners were not considered as included in the stipulation, and upon their being brought into camp an awful scene ensued.

An old squaw, infuriated by the loss of friends, or perhaps excited by the sanguinary scenes around her, seemed possessed by a demoniac ferocity. Seizing a stable fork she assaulted one miserable victim, already groaning and writhing in the agony of wounds aggravated by the scorching beams of the sun. With a delicacy of feeling scarcely to have been expected under such circumstances, Wau-bee-nee-mah stretched a mat across two poles, between me and this dreadful scene. I was thus in some degree shielded from its horrors, though I could not close my ears to the cries of the sufferer. The following night five more of the wounded prisoners were tomahawked.

After the first attack, it appears the Americans charged upon a band of Indians concealed in a sort of ravine between the sand banks and the prairie. The Indians gathered together, and after hard fighting, in which the number of whites was reduced to twenty-eight, their band succeeded in breaking through the enemy and gaining a rise of ground not far from Oak Woods. Further contest now seeming hopeless, Lieutenant Helm sent Peresh Leclerc, the half-breed boy in the service of Mr. Kinzie, who had accompanied the troops and fought manfully on their side, to propose terms of capitulation. It was stipulated, as told in Mrs. Helm's narrative, that the lives of all the survivors should be spared, and a ransom permitted as soon as practicable.

But in the meantime horrible scenes had indeed been enacted. During the engagement near the sand hills one young savage climbed into the baggage wagon which sheltered the twelve children of the white families, and tomahawked the entire group. Captain Wells, who was fighting near, beheld the deed, and exclaimed:

"Is that their game, butchering the women and children? Then I will kill, too!"

So saying, he turned his horse's head and started for the Indian camp, near the fort, where the braves had left their squaws and children.

Several Indians followed him as he galloped along. Lying flat on the neck of his horse, and loading and firing in that position, he turned occasionally on his pursuers. But at length their balls took effect, killing his horse, and severely wounding the Captain. At this moment he was met by Winnemeg and Wauban-see, who endeavoured to save him from the savages who had now overtaken him. As they helped him along, after having disengaged him from his horse, he received his deathblow from Pee-so-tum, who stabbed him in the back.

The heroic resolution shown during the fight by the wife of one of the soldiers, a Mrs. Corbin, deserves to be recorded. She had from the first expressed the determination never to fall into the hands of the savages, believing that their prisoners were invariably subjected to tortures worse than death.

When, therefore, a party came upon her to make her prisoner, she fought with desperation, refusing to surrender, although assured, by signs, of safety and kind treatment. Literally, she suffered herself to be cut to pieces, rather than become their captive.

There was a Sergeant Holt, who early in the engagement received a ball in the neck. Finding himself badly wounded, he gave his sword to his wife, who was on horseback near him, telling her to defend herself. He then made for the lake, to keep out of the way of the balls.

Mrs. Holt rode a very fine horse, which the Indians were desirous of possessing, and they therefore attacked her in the hope of dismounting her. They fought only with the butt ends of their guns, for their object was not to kill her. She hacked and hewed at their pieces as they were thrust against her, now on this side, now that. Finally, she broke loose and dashed out into the prairie, where the Indians pursued her, shouting and laughing, and now and then calling out, "The brave woman! do not hurt her!"

At length they overtook her, and while she was engaged with two or three in front, one succeeded in seizing her by the neck from behind, and in dragging her from her horse, large and powerful woman though she was. Notwithstanding their guns had been so hacked and injured, and they themselves severely cut, her captors seemed to regard her only with admiration. They took her to a trader on the Illinois River, who showed her every kindness during her captivity, and later restored her to her friends.

Meanwhile those of Mr. Kinzie's family who had remained in the boat, near the mouth of the river, were carefully guarded by Kee-po-tah and another Indian. They had seen the smoke, then the blaze, and immediately after, the report of the first tremendous discharge had sounded in their ears. Then all was confusion. They knew nothing of the events of the battle until they saw an Indian coming towards them from the battle ground, leading a horse on which sat a lady, apparently wounded.

"That is Mrs. Heald," cried Mrs. Kinzie. "That Indian will kill her. Run, Chandonnai," to one of Mr. Kinzie's clerks, "take the mule that is tied there, and offer it to him to release her."

Mrs. Heald's captor, by this time, was in the act of disengaging her bonnet from her head, in order to scalp her. Chandonnai ran up and offered the mule as a ransom, with the promise of ten bottles of whisky as soon as they should reach his village. The whisky was a strong temptation.

"But," said the Indian, "she is badly wounded—she will die. Will you give me the whisky at all events?"

Chandonnai promised that he would, and the bargain was concluded. The savage placed the lady's bonnet on his own head, and, after an ineffectual effort on the part of some squaws to rob her of her shoes and stockings, she was brought on board the boat, where she lay moaning with pain from the many bullet wounds in her arms.

Having wished to possess themselves of her horse uninjured, the Indians had aimed their shots so as to disable the rider, without in any way harming her steed.

Mrs. Heald had not lain long in the boat when a young Indian of savage aspect was seen approaching. A buffalo robe was hastily drawn over her, and she was admonished to suppress all sound of complaint, as she valued her life.

The heroic woman remained perfectly silent while the savage drew near. He had a pistol in his hand, which he rested on the side of the boat, while, with a fearful scowl, he looked pryingly around. Black Jim, one of the servants, who stood in the bow of the boat, seized an ax that lay near and signed to him that if he shot he would cleave his skull, telling him that the boat contained only the family of Shaw-nee-aw-kee. Upon this, the Indian retired. It afterwards appeared that the object of his search was Mr. Burnett, a trader from St. Joseph with whom he had some account to settle.

When the boat was at length permitted to return to the house of Mr. Kinzie, and Mrs. Heald was removed there, it became necessary to dress her wounds.

Mr. Kinzie applied to an old chief who stood by, and who, like most of his tribe, possessed some skill in surgery, to extract a ball from the arm of the sufferer.

"No, father," replied the Indian. "I cannot do it—it makes me sick here," placing his hand on his heart.

Mr. Kinzie himself then performed the operation with his penknife.

At their own house, the family of Mr. Kinzie were closely guarded by their Indian friends, whose intention it was to carry them to Detroit for security. The rest of the prisoners remained at the *wigwams* of their captors.

On the following morning, the work of plunder being completed, the Indians set fire to the fort. A very equitable distribution of the finery appeared to have been made, and shawls, ribbons, and feathers fluttered about in all directions. The ludicrous appearance of one young fellow arrayed in a muslin gown and a lady's bonnet would, under other circumstances, have been a matter of great amusement.

Black Partridge, Wau-ban-see, and Kee-po-tah, with two other Indians, established themselves in the porch of the Kinzie house as sentinels, to protect the family from any evil that the young men might be incited to commit, and all remained tranquil for a short space after the conflagration.

Very soon, however, a party of Indians from the Wabash made their appearance. These were, decidedly, the most hostile and implacable of all the tribes of the Potowatomi.

Being more remote, they had shared less than some of their brethren in the kindness of Mr. Kinzie and his family, and consequently their friendly regard was not so strong.

Runners had been sent to the villages to apprise these Indians of the intended evacuation of the post, as well as of the plan to attack the troops.

Thirsting to participate in such an event, they had hurried to the scene, and great was their mortification, on arriving at the river Aux Plaines, to meet a party of their friends with their chief, Nee-scot-nee-meg, badly wounded, and learn that the battle was over, the spoils divided, and the scalps all taken. Arriving at Chicago they blackened their faces, and proceeded toward the dwelling of Mr. Kinzie.

From his station on the *piazza* Black Partridge had watched their approach, and his fears were particularly awakened for the safety of Mrs. Helm, Mr. Kinzie's stepdaughter, who had recently come to the post, and was personally unknown to the

51

more remote Indians. By his advice she was made to assume the ordinary dress of a Frenchwoman of the country—a short gown and petticoat with a blue cotton handkerchief wrapped around her head. In this disguise she was conducted by Black Partridge himself to the house of Ouilmette, a Frenchman with a half-breed wife, who formed a part of the establishment of Mr. Kinzie and whose dwelling was close at hand.

It so happened that the Indians came first to this house in their search for prisoners. As they approached, the inmates, fearful that the fair complexion and general appearance of Mrs. Helm might betray her as an American, raised a large feather bed and placed her under the edge of it upon the bedstead, with her face to the wall. Mrs. Bisson, a half-breed sister of Ouilmette's wife, then seated herself with her sewing upon the front of the bed.

It was a hot day in August, and the feverish excitement of fear and agitation, together with her position, which was nearly suffocating, became so intolerable that Mrs. Helm at length entreated to be released and given up to the Indians.

"I can but die," said she; "let them put an end to my misery at once."

Mrs. Bisson replied, "Your death would be the destruction of us all, for Black Partridge has resolved that if one drop of the blood of your family is spilled, he will take the lives of all concerned in it, even his nearest friends; and if once the work of murder commences, there will be no end of it, so long as there remains one white person or half-breed in the country."

This expostulation nerved Mrs. Helm with fresh courage.

The Indians entered, and from her hiding place she could occasionally see them gliding about and stealthily inspecting every part of the room, though without making any ostensible search, until, apparently satisfied that there was no one concealed, they left the house.

All this time Mrs. Bisson had kept her seat upon the side of the bed, calmly sorting and arranging the patchwork of the quilt on which she was engaged, and preserving an appearance of the utmost tranquillity, although she knew not but that the next moment she might receive a tomahawk in her brain. Her self-command unquestionably saved the lives of all who were present.

From Ouilmette's house the party of Indians proceeded to the dwelling of Mr. Kinzie. They entered the parlor in which the family were assembled with their faithful protectors, and seated themselves upon the floor, in silence.

Black Partridge perceived from their moody and revengeful looks what was passing in their minds, but he dared not remonstrate with them. He only observed in a low tone to Wauban-see, "We have endeavoured to save our friends, but it is in vain—nothing will save them now."

At this moment a friendly whoop was heard from a party of newcomers on the opposite bank of the river. As the canoes in which they had hastily embarked touched the bank near the house, Black Partridge sprang to meet their leader.

"Who are you?" demanded he.

"A man. Who are you?"

"A man like yourself. But tell me who you are,"—meaning, Tell me your disposition, and which side you are for.

"I am a Sau-ga-nash!"

"Then make all speed to the house—your friend is in danger, and you alone can save him."

Billy Caldwell,[8] for it was he, entered the parlour with a calm step, and without a trace of agitation in his manner. He deliberately took off his accoutrements and placed them with his rifle behind the door, then saluted the hostile savages.

"How now, my friends! A good day to you. I was told there were enemies here, but I am glad to find only friends. Why have you blackened your faces? Is it that you are mourning for the friends you have lost in battle?" purposely misunderstanding this token of evil designs. "Or is it that you are fasting? If so, ask our friend, here, and he will give you to eat. He is the Indian's friend,

---

8. Billy Caldwell was a half-breed, and a chief of the nation. In his reply, "I am a Sau-ga-nash," or Englishman, he designed to convey, "I am a white man." Had he said, "I am a Potowatomi," it would have been interpreted to mean, "I belong to my nation, and am prepared to go all lengths with them."

and never yet refused them what they had need of."

Thus taken by surprise, the savages were ashamed to acknowledge their bloody purpose. They, therefore, said modestly that they had come to beg of their friends some white cotton in which to wrap their dead before interring them. This was given to them, with some other presents, and they peaceably took their departure from the premises.

With Mr. Kinzie's party was a non-commissioned officer who had made his escape in a singular manner. As the troops had been about to leave the fort, it was found that the baggage horses of the surgeon had strayed off. The quartermaster sergeant, Griffith, was sent to find and bring them on, it being absolutely necessary to recover them, since their packs contained part of the surgeon's apparatus and the medicines for the march.

For a long time Griffith had been on the sick report and for this reason was given charge of the baggage, instead of being placed with the troops. His efforts to recover the horses proved unsuccessful, and, alarmed at certain appearances of disorder and hostile intention among the Indians, he was hastening to rejoin his party when he was met and made prisoner by To-pee-nee-bee.

Having taken his arms and accoutrements from him, the chief put him into a canoe and paddled him across the river, bidding him make for the woods and secrete himself. This Griffith did; and in the afternoon of the following day, seeing from his lurking place that all appeared quiet, he ventured to steal cautiously into Ouilmette's garden, where he concealed himself for a time behind some currant bushes.

At length he determined to enter the house, and accordingly climbed up through a small back window into the room where the family were, entering just as the Wabash Indians had left the house of Ouilmette for that of Mr. Kinzie. The danger of the sergeant was now imminent. The family stripped him of his uniform and arrayed him in a suit of deerskin, with belt, *moccasins*, and pipe, like a French *engagé*. His dark complexion and heavy black whiskers favoured the disguise. The family were all ordered to address him in French, and, although utterly ignorant of this language, he continued to pass for a *Weem-tee-gosh*,[9] and as such remained with Mr. Kinzie and his family, undetected by his enemies, until they reached a place of safety.

On the third day after the battle, Mr. Kinzie and his family, with the clerks of the establishment, were put into a boat, under the care of François, a half-breed interpreter, and conveyed to St. Joseph, where they remained until the following November, under the protection of To-pee-nee-bee's band. With the exception of Mr. Kinzie they were then conducted to Detroit, under the escort of Chandonnai and their trusty Indian friend, Kee-po-tah, and delivered as prisoners of war to Colonel McKee, the British Indian Agent.

Mr. Kinzie himself was held at St. Joseph and did not succeed in rejoining his family until some months later. On his arrival at Detroit he was paroled by General Proctor.

Lieutenant Helm, who was likewise wounded, was carried by some friendly Indians to their village on the Au Sable and thence to Peoria, where he was liberated through the intervention of Mr. Thomas Forsyth, the half brother of Mr. Kinzie. Mrs. Helm accompanied her parents to St. Joseph, where they resided for several months in the family of Alexander Robinson,[10] receiving from them all possible kindness and hospitality.

Later Mrs. Helm was joined by her husband in Detroit, where they both were arrested by order of the British commander, and sent on horseback, in the dead of winter, through Canada to Fort George on the Niagara frontier. When they arrived at that post, there had been no official appointed to receive them, and, notwithstanding their long and fatiguing journey in the coldest, most inclement weather, Mrs. Helm, a delicate woman of seventeen years, was permitted to sit waiting in her saddle, outside the gate, for more than an hour, before the refreshment of fire or food, or even the shelter of a roof, was offered her.

When Colonel Sheaffe, who was absent at the time, was in-

---

9. Frenchman.
10. The Potowatomi chief, so well known to many of the early citizens of Chicago.

formed of this brutal inhospitality, he expressed the greatest indignation. He waited on Mrs. Helm immediately, apologized in the most courteous manner, and treated both her and Lieutenant Helm with the greatest consideration and kindness, until, by an exchange of prisoners, they were liberated and found means of reaching their friends in Steuben County, N.Y.

Captain and Mrs. Heald were sent across the lake to St. Joseph the day after the battle. The captain had received two wounds in the engagement, his wife seven.

Captain Heald had been taken prisoner by an Indian from the Kankakee, who had a strong personal regard for him, and who, when he saw Mrs. Heald's wounded and enfeebled state, released her husband that he might accompany her to St. Joseph. To the latter place they were accordingly carried by Chandonnai and his party. In the meantime, the Indian who had so nobly released his prisoner returned to his village on the Kankakee, where he had the mortification of finding that his conduct had excited great dissatisfaction among his band. So great was the displeasure manifested that he resolved to make a journey to St. Joseph and reclaim his prisoner.

News of his intention being brought to To-pee-nee-bee and Kee-po-tah, under whose care the prisoners were, they held a private council with Chandonnai, Mr. Kinzie, and the principal men of the village, the result of which was a determination to send Captain and Mrs. Heald to the Island of Mackinac and deliver them up to the British.

They were accordingly put in a bark canoe, and paddled by Robinson and his wife a distance of three hundred miles along the coast of Michigan, and surrendered as prisoners of war to the commanding officer at Mackinac.

As an instance of Captain Heald's procrastinating spirit it may be mentioned that, even after he had received positive word that his Indian captor was on the way from the Kankakee to St. Joseph to retake him, he would still have delayed at that place another day, to make preparation for a more comfortable journey to Mackinac.

The soldiers from Fort Dearborn, with their wives and surviving children, were dispersed among the different villages of the Potowatomi upon the Illinois, Wabash, and Rock rivers, and at Milwaukee, until the following spring, when the greater number of them were carried to Detroit and ransomed.

Mrs. Burns, with her infant, became the prisoner of a chief, who carried her to his village and treated her with great kindness. His wife, from jealousy of the favour shown to "the white woman" and her child, always treated them with great hostility. On one occasion she struck the infant with a tomahawk, and barely failed in her attempt to put it to death.[11] Mrs. Burns and her child were not left long in the power of the old squaw after this demonstration, but on the first opportunity were carried to a place of safety.

The family of Mr. Lee had resided in a house on the lake shore, not far from the fort. Mr. Lee was the owner of Lee's Place, which he cultivated as a farm. It was his son who had run down with the discharged soldier to give the alarm of "Indians," at the fort, on the afternoon of April 7. The father, the son, and all the other members of the family except Mrs. Lee and her young infant had fallen victims to the Indians on August 15. The two survivors were claimed by Black Partridge, and carried by him to his village on the Au Sable. He had been particularly attached to a little twelve-year-old girl of Mrs. Lee's. This child had been placed on horseback for the march; and, as she was unaccustomed to riding, she was tied fast to the saddle, lest she should slip or be thrown off.

She was within reach of the balls at the commencement of the engagement, and was severely wounded. The horse, setting off at a full gallop, partly threw her; but held fast by the bands which confined her, she hung dangling as the animal ran wildly about. In this state she was met by Black Partridge, who caught the horse and disengaged the child from the saddle. Finding her

---

11. Twenty-two years after this, as I (Mrs. Juliette A. Kinzie) was on a journey to Chicago in the steamer *Uncle Sam*, a young woman, hearing my name, introduced herself to me, and, raising the hair from her forehead, showed me the mark of the tomahawk which had so nearly been fatal to her.

so badly wounded that she could not recover, and seeing that she was in great agony, he at once put an end to her pain with his tomahawk. This, he afterwards said, was the hardest thing he had ever done, but he did it because he could not bear to see the child suffer.

Black Partridge soon became warmly attached to the mother—so much so, that he wished to marry her; and, though she very naturally objected, he continued to treat her with the greatest respect and consideration. He was in no hurry to release her, for he was still in hopes of prevailing upon her to become his wife. In the course of the winter her child fell ill. Finding that none of the remedies within their reach was effectual, Black Partridge proposed to take the little one to Chicago, to a French trader then living in the house of Mr. Kinzie, and procure medical aid from him. Wrapping up his charge with the greatest care, he set out on his journey.

Arriving at the residence of M. Du Pin, he entered the room where the Frenchman was, and carefully placed his burden on the floor.

"What have you there?" asked M. Du Pin.

"A young raccoon, which I have brought you as a present," was the reply; and, opening the pack, he showed the little sick infant.

When the trader had prescribed for the child, and Black Partridge was about to return to his home, he told his friend of the proposal he had made to Mrs. Lee to become his wife, and the manner in which it had been received.

M. Du Pin entertained some fear that the chief's honourable resolution to allow the lady herself to decide whether or not to accept his addresses might not hold out, and at once entered into a negotiation for her ransom. So effectually were the good feelings of Black Partridge wrought upon that he consented to bring his fair prisoner to Chicago immediately, that she might be restored to her friends.

Whether the kind trader had at the outset any other feeling in the matter than sympathy and brotherly kindness, we cannot

The old Kinzie house

say; we only know that in course of time Mrs. Lee became Madame Du Pin, and that the worthy couple lived together in great happiness for many years after.

The fate of Nau-non-gee, a chief of the Calumet village, deserves to be recorded.

During the battle of August 15, the principal object of his attack was one Sergeant Hays, a man from whom he had accepted many kindnesses.

After Hays had received a ball through the body, this Indian ran up to tomahawk him, when the sergeant, summoning his remaining strength, pierced him through the body with his bayonet. The two fell together. Other Indians running up soon dispatched Hays, and not until then was his bayonet extracted from the body of his adversary.

After the battle the wounded chief was carried to his village on the Calumet, where he survived for several days. Finding his end approaching, he called together his young men, and enjoined them, in the most solemn manner, to regard the safety of their prisoners after his death, and out of respect to his memory to take the lives of none of them; for he himself fully deserved his fate at the hands of the man whose kindness he had so ill requited.

John Kinzie: A Sketch

John McKenzie, or, as he was afterwards called, John Kinzie, was the son of Surgeon John McKenzie of the 60th Royal American Regiment of Foot, and of Anne Haleyburton, the widow of Chaplain William Haleyburton of the First or Royal American Regiment of Foot.

Major Haleyburton died soon after their arrival in America, and two years later his widow married Surgeon John McKenzie. Their son John was born in Quebec, December 3, 1763.

In the old family Bible the "Mc" is dropped in recording the birth of "John Kinsey" (so spelled), thus indicating that he was known as John Kinsey, or, as he himself spelled it, "Kinzie," from early childhood.

Major McKenzie survived the birth of his son but a few months, and his widow took for her third husband Mr. William Forsyth, of New York City.

Young John grew up under the care and supervision of his stepfather, Mr. Forsyth, until at the age of ten he began his adventurous career by running away.

He and his two half brothers attended a school at Williamsburg, L. I., escorted there every Monday by a servant, who came to take them home every Friday. One fine afternoon when the servant came for the boys Master Johnny was missing. An immediate search was made, but not a trace of him could be found. His mother was almost frantic. The mysterious disappearance of her bright, handsome boy was a fearful blow.

Days passed without tidings of the lost one, and hope fled.

The only solution suggested was, that he might have been accidentally drowned and his body swept out to sea.

Meantime Master John was very much alive.

He had determined to go to Quebec to try, as he afterwards explained, to discover some of his father's relatives.

He had managed to find a sloop which was just going up the Hudson, and with the confidence and audacity of a child, stepped gaily on board and set forth on his travels.

Most fortunately for him, he attracted the notice of a passenger who was going to Quebec, and who began to question the lonely little lad. He became so interested in the boy that he took him in charge, paid his fare, and landed him safely in his native city.

But here, alas, Master Johnny soon found himself stranded. Very cold, very hungry, and very miserable, he was wandering down one of the streets of Quebec when his attention was attracted by a glittering array of watches and silver in a shop window, where a man was sitting repairing a clock.

Johnny stood gazing wistfully in. His yellow curls, blue eyes, and pathetic little face appealed to the kind silversmith, who beckoned him into the shop and soon learned his story.

"And what are you going to do now?" asked the man.

"I am going to work," replied ten-year-old valiantly.

"Why, what could you do?" laughed the man.

"I could do anything you told me to do, if you just showed me how to do it," said John.

The result was that John got a job.

The silversmith had no children, and as the months rolled on he grew more and more fond of John. He taught him as much of his trade as the lad could acquire in the three years of his stay in Quebec. Later in his life this knowledge was of great value to him, for it enabled him to secure the friendship and assistance of the Indians by fashioning for them various ornaments and "tokens" from the silver money paid them as annuities by the United States Government. The Indians called him "Shaw-nee-aw-kee" or the Silver Man, and by that name he was known among all the tribes of the Northwest.

These happy and useful years drew to a close. As John was one day walking down the street, a gentleman from New York stopped him and said: "Are you not Johnny Kinzie?" John admitted that he was, and the gentleman, armed with the astonishing news and the boy's address, promptly communicated with Mr. Forsyth, who at once came to Quebec and took the runaway home.

His rejoicing mother doubtless saved him from the sound thrashing he richly deserved at the hands of his stepfather.

John had now had enough of running away, and was content to stay at home and buckle down to his books. The few letters of his which remain and are preserved in the Chicago Historical Society give evidence of an excellent education.

The roving spirit was still alive in him, however. Mr. Forsyth had moved West and settled in Detroit, and when John was about eighteen years old he persuaded his stepfather to fit him out as an Indian trader.

This venture proved a great success. Before he was one and twenty, young Kinzie had established two trading posts, one at Sandusky and one at Maumee, and was pushing towards the west, where he later started a depot at St. Joseph, Michigan.

John Kinzie's success as an Indian trader was almost phenomenal. He acquired the language of the Indians with great facility; he respected their customs, and they soon found that his "word was as good as his bond." He was a keen trader, not allowing himself to be cheated, nor attempting to cheat the Indians. He quickly gained the confidence and esteem of the various tribes with which he dealt, and the personal friendship of many of their most powerful chiefs, who showed themselves ready to shield him in danger, and to rescue him from harm at the risk of their lives.

When in the neighbourhood of Detroit, he stayed with his half brother, William Forsyth, who had married a Miss Margaret Lytle, daughter of Colonel William Lytle of Virginia. In their home he was always a welcome guest; and here he met Mrs.

Forsyth's younger sister, Eleanor. She was the widow of a British officer, Captain Daniel McKillip, who had been killed in a sortie from Ft. Defiance. Since her husband's death, she and her little daughter Margaret had made their home with the Forsyths.

John Kinzie fell desperately in love with the handsome young widow, and on January 23, 1798, they were married.

In all of his new and arduous career he had been greatly aided and protected by John Harris, the famous Indian scout and trader mentioned by Irving in his *Life of Washington* (Volume 1, Chapter 12). It was in grateful appreciation of these kindnesses that he named his son "John Harris," after this valued friend.

Mr. Kinzie continued to extend his business still farther west, until in October, 1803, when his son John Harris was but three months old, he moved with his family to Chicago, where he purchased the trading establishment of a Frenchman named Le Mai.

Here, cut off from the world at large, with no society but the garrison at Fort Dearborn, the Kinzies lived in contentment, and in the quiet enjoyment of all the comforts, together with many of the luxuries of life. The first white child born outside of Fort Dearborn was their little daughter Ellen Marion, on December 20, 1805. Next came Maria, born September 28, 1807. Then, last, Robert Allan, born February 8, 1810.

By degrees, Mr. Kinzie established still more remote posts, all contributing to the parent post at Chicago; at Milwaukee, with the Menominee; at Rock River with the Winnebago and the Potowatomi; on the Illinois River and the Kankakee with the Prairie Potowatomi; and with the Kickapoo in what was called "Le Large," the widely extended district afterwards converted into Sangamon County. He was appointed Sub-Indian Agent and Government Interpreter, and in these capacities rendered valuable service.

About the year 1810, a Frenchman named Lalime was killed by John Kinzie under the following circumstances: Lalime had become insanely jealous of Mr. Kinzie's success as a rival trader, and was unwise enough to threaten to take Kinzie's life. The latter only laughed at the reports, saying "Threatened men live long, and I am not worrying over Lalime's wild talk." Several of his stanchest Indian friends, however, continued to warn him, and he at last consented to carry some sort of weapon in case Lalime really had the folly to attack him. He accordingly took a carving knife from the house and began sharpening it on a grindstone in the woodshed.

Young John stood beside him, much interested in this novel proceeding.

"What are you doing, father?" he asked.

"Sharpening this knife, my son," was the reply.

"What for?" said John.

"Go into the house," replied his father, "and don't ask questions about things that don't concern you."

A few days passed. Nothing happened; but Mr. Kinzie carried the knife.

Mrs. Kinzie's daughter by her first marriage was now seventeen years old, and was the wife of Lieutenant Linai Thomas Helm, one of the officers stationed at Fort Dearborn, and Mr. Kinzie frequently went over there to spend the evening. One very dark night he sauntered over to the fort, and was just entering the inclosure, when a man sprang out from behind the gate post and plunged a knife into his neck. It was Lalime. Quick as a flash, Mr. Kinzie drew his own knife and dealt Lalime a furious blow, and a fatal one. The man fell like a log into the river below. Mr. Kinzie staggered home, covered with blood from the deep wound.

The late Gurdon S. Hubbard, in a letter to a grandson of John Kinzie's, gives the following account of the affair:

143 Locust St., Chicago, Ill.,
Feb. 6th, 1884.

Arthur M. Kinzie, Esq.,
My Dear Sir,
I have yours of 5th. You corroborate what I have said about your grandfather killing Lalime as far as you state. I am glad you do. I cannot forget what I heard from your

grandmother and Mrs. Helm. They said your grandfather, coming in bloody, said "I have killed Lalime. A guard will be sent from the fort to take me. Dress my neck quickly!" Your grandmother did so, remarking "They shall not take you to the fort—come with me to the woods." She hid him, came home, and soon a sergeant with guard appeared. Could not find your grandfather.

After the excitement was over, the officers began to reason on the subject calmly, for Lalime was highly respected, good social company, educated. They came to the conclusion that the act was in self defence. The history of Chicago, by Mr. Andreas will soon be out. He sent me the account relating to your grandfather to revise. Much in it incorrect, which I have explained.

Can't you come and see me?

Your friend,

G. S. Hubbard.

As far as it goes this account agrees with the facts as held by the family. The Kinzies, however, always stated that after the excitement subsided, as it did in a few weeks, Mr. Kinzie sent word to the commanding officer at the fort that he wished to come in, give himself up, and have a fair trial. This was granted. The fresh wounds in his neck—the thrust had barely missed the jugular vein—and the testimony given as to the threats Lalime had uttered, resulted in an immediate verdict of justifiable homicide.

In the meantime some of Lalime's friends conceived the idea that it would be a suitable punishment for Mr. Kinzie to bury his victim directly in front of the Kinzie home, where he must necessarily behold the grave every time he passed out of his own gate. Great was their chagrin and disappointment, however, when Mr. Kinzie, far from being annoyed at their action, proceeded to make Lalime's grave his special care.

Flowers were planted on it and it was kept in most beautiful order. Many a half hour the Kinzie children longed to spend in play, was occupied by their father's order in raking the dead leaves away from Lalime's grave and watering the flowers there.

About two years subsequent to this event the Fort Dearborn Massacre occurred. John Kinzie's part in that tragedy has already been given in Helm's narrative.

After the massacre Mr. Kinzie was not allowed to leave St. Joseph with his family, his Indian friends insisting that he remain and endeavour to secure some remnant of his scattered property. During his excursions with them for that purpose he wore the costume and paint of the tribe in order to escape capture and perhaps death at the hands of those who were still thirsting for blood.

His anxiety for his family at length became so great that he followed them to Detroit, where he was paroled by General Proctor in January.

At the surrender of Detroit, which took place the day before the massacre at Chicago, General Hull had stipulated that the inhabitants should be permitted to remain undisturbed in their homes. Accordingly, the family of Mr. Kinzie took up their residence among their friends in the old mansion which many will recollect as standing on the northwest corner of Jefferson Avenue and Wayne Street, Detroit.

Feelings of indignation and sympathy were constantly aroused in the hearts of the citizens during the winter that ensued. They were almost daily called upon to witness the cruelties practiced upon American prisoners brought in by their Indian captors. Those who could scarcely drag their wounded, bleeding feet over the frozen ground were compelled to dance for the amusement of the savages; and these exhibitions sometimes took place before the Government House, the residence of Colonel McKee. Sometimes British officers looked on from their windows at these heart-rending performances. For the honour of humanity, we will hope such instances were rare.

Everything available among the effects of the citizens was offered to ransom their countrymen from the hands of these inhuman beings. The prisoners brought in from the River Raisin—those unfortunate men who were permitted, after their surrender to General Proctor, to be tortured and murdered by inches by his savage allies—excited the sympathy and called for the action of the whole community. Private houses were turned into hospitals, and everyone was forward to get possession of as many as possible of the survivors. To accomplish this, even articles of apparel were bartered by the ladies of Detroit, as from doors or windows they watched the miserable victims carried about for sale.

In the dwelling of Mr. Kinzie one large room was devoted to the reception of the sufferers. Few of them survived. Among those spoken of as arousing the deepest interest were two young gentlemen of Kentucky, brothers, both severely wounded, and their wounds aggravated to a mortal degree by subsequent ill usage and hardships. Their solicitude for each other, and their exhibition in various ways of the most tender fraternal affection, created an impression never to be forgotten.

The last bargain made by the Kinzies was effected by black Jim and one of the children, who had permission to redeem a negro servant of the gallant Colonel Allen with an old white horse, the only available article that remained among their possessions. A brother of Colonel Allen's afterwards came to Detroit, and the negro preferred returning to servitude rather than remaining a stranger in a strange land.

Mr. Kinzie, as has been related, joined his family at Detroit in the month of January. A short time after his arrival suspicion arose in the mind of General Proctor that he was in correspondence with General Harrison, who was now at Fort Meigs, and who was believed to be meditating an advance upon Detroit. Lieutenant Watson, of the British army, waited upon Mr. Kinzie one day with an invitation to the quarters of General Proctor on the opposite side of the river, saying the general wished to speak with him on business.

Quite unsuspecting, Mr. Kinzie complied with the request, when to his surprise he was ordered into confinement, and strictly guarded in the house of his former partner, Mr. Patterson, of Sandwich.

Finding he did not return home, Mrs. Kinzie informed some Indian chiefs, Mr. Kinzie's particular friends, who immediately repaired to the headquarters of the commanding officer, demanded "their friend's" release, and brought him back to his home. After waiting until a favourable opportunity presented itself, the general sent a detachment of dragoons to arrest Mr. Kinzie. They succeeded in carrying him away, and crossing the river with him. Just at this moment a party of friendly Indians made their appearance.

"Where is Shaw-nee-aw-kee?" was the first question.

"There," replied his wife, pointing across the river, "in the hands of the redcoats, who are taking him away again."

The Indians ran down to the river, seized some canoes they found there, and, crossing over to Sandwich, a second time compelled General Proctor to forego his intentions.

A third time this officer attempted to imprison Mr. Kinzie, and this time succeeded in conveying him heavily ironed to Fort Malden, in Canada, at the mouth of the Detroit River. Here he was at first treated with great severity, but after a time the rigor of his confinement was somewhat relaxed, and he was permitted to walk on the bank of the river for air and exercise.

On September 10, as he was taking his promenade under the close supervision of a guard of soldiers, the whole party were startled by the sound of guns upon Lake Erie, at no great distance below. What could it mean? It must be Commodore Barclay firing into some of the Yankees. The firing continued.

The hour allotted to the prisoner for his daily walk expired, but neither he nor his guard observed the lapse of time, so anxiously were they listening to what they now felt sure must be an engagement between ships of war. At length Mr. Kinzie was reminded that he must return to confinement. He petitioned for another half hour.

"Let me stay," said he, "till we can learn how the battle has gone."

Very soon a sloop appeared under press of sail, rounding the point, and presently two gunboats in pursuit of her.

"She is running—she bears the British colours!" cried Kinzie. "Yes, yes, they are lowering—she is striking her flag! Now," turning to the soldiers, "I will go back to prison contented—I know how the battle has gone."

The sloop was the *Little Belt*, the last of the squadron captured by the gallant Perry on that memorable occasion which he announced in the immortal words:

"We have met the enemy, and they are ours."

Matters were growing critical, and it was necessary to transfer all prisoners to a place of greater security than the frontier was now likely to be. It was resolved, therefore, to send Mr. Kinzie to the mother country.

Nothing has ever appeared which would in any way explain the course of General Proctor in regard to this gentleman. He had been taken from the bosom of his family, where he was living quietly under the parole he had received, protected by the stipulations of the surrender. For months he had been kept in confinement. Now he was placed on horseback under a strong guard, who announced that they had orders to shoot him through the head if he offered to speak to a person upon the road. He was tied upon the saddle to prevent his escape, and thus set out for Quebec. A little incident occurred which will illustrate the course invariably pursued towards our citizens at this period by the British Army on the Northwestern frontier.

The saddle on which Mr. Kinzie rode had not been properly fastened, and, owing to the rough motion of the animal it turned, bringing the rider into a most awkward and painful position. His limbs being fastened, he could not disengage himself, and in this manner he was compelled to ride until nearly exhausted, before those in charge had the humanity to release him.

Arrived at Quebec, he was put on board a small vessel to be sent to England. When a few days out at sea the vessel was chased by an American frigate and driven into Halifax. A second time she set sail, when she sprung a leak and was compelled to put back.

The attempt to send Mr. Kinzie across the ocean was now

abandoned, and he was returned to Quebec. Another step, equally inexplicable with his arrest, was soon after taken.

Although the War of 1812 was not yet ended, Mr. Kinzie, together with a Mr. Macomb, of Detroit, who was also in confinement in Quebec, was released and given permission to return to his friends and family. It may possibly be imagined that in the treatment these gentlemen received, the British commander-in-chief sheltered himself under the plea of their being "native born British subjects," and that perhaps when it was ascertained that Mr. Kinzie was indeed a citizen of the United States it was thought safest to release him.

In the meantime, General Harrison at the head of his troops had reached Detroit. He landed September 29. All the citizens went forth to meet him. Mrs. Kinzie, leading her children, was of the number. The general accompanied her to her home, and took up his abode there. On his arrival he was introduced to Kee-po-tah, who happened to be on a visit to the family at that time. The general had seen the chief the preceding year, at the Council at Vincennes, and the meeting was one of great cordiality and interest.

Fort Dearborn was rebuilt in 1816, on a larger scale than before, and, on the return of the troops, the bones of the unfortunate Americans who had been massacred four years previously were collected and buried.

In this same year Mr. Kinzie and his family again returned to Chicago, where he at once undertook to collect the scattered remnants of his property—a most disheartening task. He found his various trading-posts abandoned, his clerks scattered, and his valuable furs and goods lost or destroyed.

In real estate, however, he was rich—for he owned nearly all the land on the north side of the Chicago River, and many acres on the south and west sides, as well as all of what was known as "Kinzie's Addition."

At the present day the "Kinzie School," and the street which bears his name, are all that remain to remind this generation of the pioneer on whose land now stands the wonderful City of

CORNPLANTER, A SENECA CHIEF

Chicago.

Mr. Kinzie, recognizing the importance of the geographical position of Chicago, and the vast fertility of the surrounding country, had always foretold its eventual prosperity. Unfortunately, he was not permitted to witness the fulfilment of his predictions.

On January 6, 1828, he was stricken with apoplexy, and in a few hours death closed his useful and energetic career.

He lies buried in Graceland Cemetery, Chicago. Loyal in life, death has mingled his ashes with the soil of the city whose future greatness he was perhaps the first to foresee.

John Kinzie was not only the sturdy, helpful pioneer, but also the genial, courteous gentleman.

To keen business ability he united the strictest honesty, and to the most dauntless courage, a tender and generous heart.

As the devoted friend of the red man, tradition has handed down the name of Shaw-nee-aw-kee throughout all the tribes of the Northwest.

The Capture by the Indians of Little Eleanor Lytle

(Afterward the wife of John Kinzie.)

It is well known that previous to the War of the Revolution the whole of western Pennsylvania was inhabited by various Indian tribes. Of these the Delawares were the friends of the whites, and after the commencement of the great struggle took part with the United States. The Iroquois, on the contrary, were the friends and allies of the mother country.

Very few white settlers had ventured beyond the Susquehanna. The numerous roving bands of Shawano, Nanticoke, and other Indians, although at times professing friendship for the Americans and acting in concert with the Delawares or Lenape as allies, at other times suffered themselves to be seduced by their neighbours, the Iroquois, into showing a most sanguinary spirit of hostility.

For this reason the life of the settlers on the frontier was one of constant peril and alarm. Many a dismal scene of barbarity was enacted, as the history of the times testifies, and even those who felt themselves in some measure protected by their immediate neighbours, the Delawares, never lost sight of the caution required by their exposed situation.

The vicinity of the military garrison at Pittsburgh, or Fort Pitt, as it was then called, gave additional security to those who had pushed farther west among the fertile valleys of the Allegheny and Monongahela. Among these was the family of Mr. Lytle, who, some years previous to the opening of our story, had removed from Baltimore to Path Valley, near Carlisle, and subsequently had settled on the banks of Plum River, a tributary of the Allegheny. Here, with his wife and five children, he had lived in comfort and security, undisturbed by any hostile visit, and annoyed only by occasional false alarms from his more timorous neighbours, who, having had sad experience in frontier life, were prone to anticipate evil, and magnify every appearance of danger.

On a bright afternoon in the autumn of 1779, two of Mr. Lytle's children, a girl of eight and her brother, two years younger, were playing in a little hollow in the rear of their father's house. Some large trees which had recently been felled were lying here and there, still untrimmed, and many logs, prepared for fuel, were scattered around. Upon one of these logs the children, wearied with their sport, seated themselves, and fell into conversation upon a subject that greatly perplexed them.

While playing in the same place a few hours previous, they had imagined they saw an Indian lurking behind one of the fallen trees. The Indians of the neighbourhood were in the habit of making occasional visits to the family, and the children had become familiar and even affectionate with many of them, but this Indian had seemed to be a stranger, and after the first hasty glance they had fled in alarm to the house.

Their mother had chid them for bringing such a report, which she had endeavoured to convince them was without foundation. "You know," said she, "you are always alarming us unnecessarily: the neighbours' children have frightened you nearly to death. Go back to your play, and learn to be more courageous."

So, hardly persuaded by their mother's arguments, the children had returned to their sports. Now as they sat upon the trunk of the tree, their discourse was interrupted by what seemed to be the note of a quail not far off.

"Listen," said the boy, as a second note answered the first; "do you hear that?"

"Yes," replied his sister, and after a few moments' silence, "do you not hear a rustling among the branches of the tree yonder?"

"Perhaps it is a squirrel—but look! what is that? Surely I saw something red among the branches. It looked like a fawn popping up its head."

At this moment, the children, who had been gazing so intently in the direction of the fallen tree that all other objects were forgotten, felt themselves seized from behind and pinioned in an iron grasp. What was their horror and dismay to find themselves in the arms of savages, whose terrific countenances and gestures plainly showed them to be enemies!

They made signs to the children to be silent, on pain of death, and hurried them off, half dead with terror, in a direction leading from their home. After travelling some distance in profound silence, their captors somewhat relaxed their severity, and as night approached the party halted, adopting the usual precautions to secure themselves against a surprise.

Torn from their beloved home and parents, in an agony of uncertainty and terror, and anticipating all the horrors with which the rumours of the times had invested captivity among the Indians—perhaps even torture and death—the poor children could no longer restrain their grief, but gave vent to sobs and lamentations.

Their distress appeared to excite the compassion of one of the party, a man of mild aspect, who approached and endeavoured to soothe them. He spread them a couch of the long grass which grew near the camping place, offered them a portion of his own stock of dried meat and parched corn, and made them understand by signs that no further evil was intended.

These kindly demonstrations were interrupted by the arrival of another party of Indians, bringing with them the mother of the little prisoners, with her youngest child, an infant three months old.

It had so happened that early in the day the father of the family, with his serving men, had gone to a "raising" a few miles distant, and the house had thus been left without a defender. The long period of tranquillity they had enjoyed, free from all molestation or even alarm from the savages, had thrown the settlers quite off their guard, and they had recently laid aside some of the caution they had formerly deemed necessary.

By lying in wait, the Indians had found a favourable moment for seizing the defenceless family and making them prisoners. Judging from their paint and other marks by which the early settlers learned to distinguish the various tribes, Mrs. Lytle conjectured that the savages into whose hands she and her children had fallen were Senecas. Nor was she mistaken. They were a party of that tribe who had descended from their village with the intention of falling upon some isolated band of their enemies, the Delawares, but failing in this, they had made themselves amends by capturing a few white settlers.

It is to be attributed to the generally mild disposition of this tribe, together with the magnanimous character of the chief who accompanied the party, that the prisoners in the present instance escaped the fate of most of the Americans who were so unhappy as to fall into the hands of the Iroquois.

The children could learn nothing from their mother as to the fate of their other brother and sister, a boy of six and a little girl of four years of age, though she was in hopes they had escaped with the servant girl, who had likewise disappeared.

After delaying a few hours in order to revive the exhausted prisoners, the savages again started on their march, one of the older Indians offering to relieve the mother of the burden of her infant, which she had hitherto carried in her arms. Pleased with the unexpected kindness, she resigned the child to him.

Thus they pursued their way, the savage who carried the infant lingering somewhat behind the rest of the party. At last, finding a spot convenient for his evil purpose, he grasped his innocent victim by the feet and, with one whirl to add strength to the blow, dashed out its brains against a tree. Leaving the body upon the spot, he then rejoined the party.

The mother, unaware of what had happened, regarded him suspiciously as he reappeared without the child—then gazed wildly around the group. Her beloved little one was not there. Its absence spoke its fate; but, knowing the lives of her remaining children depended upon her firmness in that trying hour, she suppressed a shriek of agony and, drawing them yet closer to her, pursued her melancholy way without word or question.

From the depths of her heart she cried unto Him who is able to save, and He comforted her with hopes of deliverance for the survivors; for she saw that if blood had been the sole object of their enemies her scalp and the scalps of her children would have been taken upon the spot where they were made prisoners.

She read, too, in the eyes of one who was evidently the commander of the party an expression more merciful than she had dared to hope for. Particularly had she observed his soothing manner and manifest partiality towards her eldest child, her little Eleanor, and upon these slender foundations she built many bright hopes of either escape or ransom.

After a toilsome and painful march of many days, the party reached the Seneca village, upon the headwaters of the Allegheny, near what is now Olean Point. On their arrival their conductor, a chief distinguished by the name of the Big White Man,[1] led his prisoners to the principal lodge. This was occupied by his mother, the widow of the head chief of the band, who was called the Old Queen.

On entering her presence, her son presented the little girl, saying, "My mother, I bring you a child to take the place of my brother who was killed by the Lenape six moons ago. She shall dwell in my lodge, and be to me a sister. Take the white woman and her children and treat them kindly—our Father will give us many horses and guns to buy them back again."

He referred to the British Indian Agent of his tribe, Colonel Johnson, an excellent and benevolent gentleman, who resided at Fort Niagara, on the British side of the Niagara River.

The Old Queen carried out the injunctions of her son. She received the prisoners, and every comfort that her simple and primitive mode of life made possible was provided them.

1. Although this is the name of her benefactor, preserved by our mother, it seems evident that this chief was in fact Corn Planter, a personage well known in the history of the times. There could hardly have been two such prominent chiefs of the same name in one village.

We must now return to the time and place at which our story commences.

Late in the evening of that day the father returned to his dwelling. All around and within was silent and desolate. No trace of a living creature was to be found in the house or throughout the grounds. His nearest neighbours lived at a considerable distance, but to them he hastened, frantically demanding tidings of his family.

As he aroused them from their slumbers, one after another joined him in the search. At length, at one of the houses, the maid servant who had effected her escape was found. Her first place of refuge, she said, had been a large brewing tub in an outer kitchen, under which she had secreted herself until the Indians, who were evidently in haste, departed and gave her the opportunity of fleeing to a place of greater safety. She could give no tidings of her mistress and the children, except that they had not been murdered in her sight or hearing.

At last, having scoured the neighbourhood without success, Mr. Lytle thought of an old settler who lived alone, far up the valley. Thither he and his friends immediately repaired, and from him they learned that, while at work in his field just before sunset, he had seen a party of strange Indians passing at a short distance from his cabin. As they wound along the brow of the hill he perceived that they had prisoners with them—a woman and a child. The woman he knew to be white, as she carried her infant in her arms, instead of upon her back, after the manner of the savages.

Day had now begun to break. The night had been passed in fruitless search, and, after consultation with kind friends and neighbours, the agonized father accepted their offer to accompany him to Fort Pitt that they might ask advice and assistance of the commandant and Indian Agent there.

Proceeding down the valley, they approached a hut which the night before they had found apparently deserted, and were startled by seeing two children standing in front of it. In them the delighted father recognized two of his missing flock, but no tidings could they give him of their mother or of the other members of his family.

Their story was simple and touching. They had been playing in the garden when they were alarmed by seeing Indians enter the yard near the house. Unperceived, the brother, who was but six years of age, helped his little sister over the fence into a field overrun with wild blackberry and raspberry bushes. Among these they concealed themselves for awhile, and then, finding all quiet, attempted to force their way to the side of the field farthest from the house. Unfortunately, in her play in the garden the little girl had pulled off her shoes and stockings, and now with the briers pricking and tearing her tender feet, she could with difficulty refrain from crying out.

Her brother took off his stockings and put them on her feet, and attempted to protect her with his shoes, also; but they were too large, and kept slipping off, so that she could not wear them. For a time the children persevered in making their escape from what they considered certain death, for, as was said, they had been taught, by the tales they had heard, to regard all strange Indians as ministers of torture and of horrors worse than death. Exhausted with pain and fatigue, the poor little girl at length declared that she could not go any farther.

"Then, Maggie," said her brother, "I must kill you, for I cannot let you be killed by the Indians."

"Oh, no, Thomas!" pleaded she, "do not, do not kill me! I do not think the Indians will find us."

"Oh, yes, they will, Maggie, and I could kill you so much easier than they would!"

For a long time he endeavoured to persuade her, and even looked about for a stick sufficiently large for his purpose; but despair gave the child strength, and she promised her brother she would neither complain nor falter if he would help her make her way out of the field.

The little boy's idea that he could save his sister from savage barbarity only by taking her life shows with what tales of horror the children of the early settlers were familiar.

After a few more efforts, they made their way out of the field into an open pasture ground where, to their great delight, they saw some cows feeding. They recognized the animals as belonging to Granny Myers, an old woman who lived at some little distance from the place where they then were, but in what direction they were utterly ignorant.

With a sagacity beyond his years the boy said, "Let us hide ourselves till sunset. Then the cows will go home, and we will follow them."

This they did; but, to their dismay, when they reached Granny Myers's they found the house deserted. The old woman had been called down the valley by some business, and did not return that night.

Tired and hungry, the children could go no farther, and after an almost fruitless endeavour to get some milk from the cows, lay down to sleep under an old bedstead that stood behind the house. During the night their father and his party caused them additional terror. The shouts and calls which had been designed to arouse the inmates of the house the children mistook for the whoop of the Indians, and, unable to distinguish friends from foes, crept close to each other, as far out of sight as possible. When found the following morning, they were debating what course for safety to take next.

The commandant at Fort Pitt entered warmly into the affairs of Mr. Lytle, and readily furnished a detachment of soldiers to aid him and his friends in the pursuit of the marauders. Circumstances having thrown suspicion upon the Senecas, the party soon directed their search among the villages of that tribe.

Their inquiries were prosecuted in various directions, and always with great caution, for all the tribes of the Iroquois, or, as they pompously called themselves, the Five Nations, being allies of Great Britain, were inveterate in their hostility toward the Americans. Thus some time elapsed before the father with his assistants reached the village of the Big White Man.

Negotiations for the ransom of the captives were immediately begun and in the case of Mrs. Lytle and the younger child easily carried into effect. But no offers, no entreaties, no promises could procure the release of little Eleanor, the adopted child of the tribe. No, the chief said, she was his sister; he had taken her to supply the place of his brother who was killed by the enemy; she was dear to him, and he would not part with her.

Finding every effort to shake this resolution unavailing, the father was compelled to take his sorrowful departure with the loved ones he had had the good fortune to recover.

We will not attempt to depict the grief of parents thus compelled to give up a darling child, leaving her in the hands of savages whom until now they had had too much reason to regard as merciless. But there was no alternative; so commending her to the care of their heavenly Father, and cheered by the manifest tenderness with which she had thus far been treated, they set out on their melancholy journey homeward, trusting that some future effort for her recovery would be more effectual.

Having placed his family in safety in Pittsburgh, Mr. Lytle, still assisted by the commandant and the Indian agent, undertook an expedition to the frontier to the residence of the British agent, Colonel Johnson. His account of the case warmly interested that benevolent officer, who promised to spare no exertion in his behalf. This promise was religiously fulfilled. As soon as the opening of spring permitted, Colonel Johnson went in person to the village of the Big White Man, and offered the chief many splendid presents of guns and horses; but he was inexorable.

Time rolled on, and every year the hope of recovering the little captive became more faint. She, in the meantime, continued to wind herself more and more closely around the heart of her Indian brother. Nothing could exceed the consideration and affection with which she was treated, not only by him, but by his mother, the Old Queen. All their brooches and *wampum* were employed in the decoration of her person. The chief seat and the most delicate viands were invariably reserved for her, and no efforts were spared to promote her happiness and banish from her mind memories of her former home and kindred.

Thus, though she had beheld the departure of her parents

and her dear little brother with a feeling amounting almost to despair, and had for a long while resisted every attempt at consolation, time at length, as it ever does, brought its soothing balm, and she grew contented and happy.

From her activity and forcefulness, characteristics for which she was remarkable to the end of her life, she was given the name, "The Ship under Full Sail."

The only drawback to the happiness of the little prisoner, aside from her longing for her own dear home, was the enmity of the wife of the Big White Man. This woman, from the day of Eleanor's arrival at the village and her adoption as a sister into the family, had conceived for the child the greatest animosity, which she at first had the prudence to conceal from her husband.

It was perhaps natural that a wife should give way to some feeling of jealousy at seeing her place in the heart of her husband usurped by the child of their enemy, the American. But these feelings were aggravated by a bad and vindictive temper, as well as by the indifference with which her husband listened to her complaints and murmurings.

As the woman had no children of her own to engage her attention, her mind was the more easily engrossed and inflamed by her fancied wrongs, and the devising of means for their redress. An apparent opportunity for revenge was not long wanting.

During the absence of the Big White Man upon some war party or hunting excursion, little Eleanor was taken ill with fever and ague. She was nursed with the utmost tenderness by the Old Queen; and the wife of the chief, to lull suspicion, was likewise unwearied in her attentions to the little favourite.

One afternoon while the Old Queen was absent for a short time, her daughter-in-law entered the lodge with a bowl of something she had prepared, and, stooping down to the mat on which the child lay, said, in an affectionate tone, "Drink, my sister. I have brought you that which will drive this fever far from you."

On raising her head to reply, the little girl saw a pair of eyes

85

peeping through a crevice in the lodge, fixed upon her with a peculiar and significant expression. With the quick perception due partly to instinct and partly to her intercourse with the red people, she replied faintly, "Set it down, my sister. When this fit of the fever has passed, I will drink your medicine."

The squaw, too cautious to importune, busied herself about the lodge for a short time; then withdrew to another near at hand. Meantime the bright eyes continued to peer through the opening until they had watched the object of their gaze fairly out of sight. Then a low voice, the voice of a young friend and playfellow, spoke: "Do not drink that which your brother's wife has brought you. She hates you, and is only waiting an opportunity to rid herself of you. I have watched her all the morning, and have seen her gathering the most deadly roots and herbs. I knew for whom they were intended, and came hither to warn you."

"Take the bowl," said the little invalid, "and carry it to my mother's lodge."

This was accordingly done. The contents of the bowl were found to consist principally of a decoction of the root of the May-apple, the most deadly poison known among the Indians.

It is not in the power of language to describe the indignation that pervaded the little community when this discovery was made known. The squaws ran to and fro, as is their custom when excited, each vying with the other in heaping invectives upon the culprit. For the present, however, no further punishment was inflicted upon her, and, the first burst of rage over, she was treated with silent abhorrence.

The little patient was removed to the lodge of the Old Queen and strictly guarded, while her enemy was left to wander in silence and solitude about the fields and woods, until the return of her husband should determine her punishment.

In a few days, the excursion being over, the Big White Man and his party returned to the village. Contrary to the custom of savages, he did not, in his first passion at learning the attempt on the life of his little sister, take summary vengeance on the offender. Instead, he contented himself with banishing the squaw from his lodge, never to return, and in condemning her to hoe corn in a distant part of the large field or inclosure which served the whole community for a garden.

Although thereafter she would still show her vindictiveness toward the little girl by striking at her with her hoe, or by some other spiteful action whenever, by chance, Eleanor and her companions wandered into that vicinity, yet she was either too well watched or stood too much in awe of her former husband to repeat the attempt upon his sister's life.

Four years had now elapsed since the capture of little Nelly. Her heart was by nature warm and affectionate, and the unbounded tenderness of those among whom she dwelt called forth in her a corresponding feeling. She regarded the chief and his mother with love and reverence, and had so completely acquired their language and customs as almost to have forgotten her own.

So identified had she become with the tribe that the remembrance of her home and family had nearly faded from her mind—all but the memory of her mother, her mother, whom she had loved with a strength of affection natural to her warm and ardent disposition, and to whom her heart still clung with a fondness that no time or change could destroy.

The peace of 1783 between Great Britain and the United States was now effected, in consequence of which there was a general pacification of the Indian tribes, and fresh hopes were aroused in the bosoms of Mr. and Mrs. Lytle.

They removed with their family to Fort Niagara, near which, on the American side, was the Great Council Fire of the Senecas. Colonel Johnson again readily undertook negotiations with the chief in their behalf, and, in order to lose no chance of success, he again proceeded in person to the village of the Big White Man.

His visit was most opportune. He arrived among the Senecas during the Feast of the Green Corn. This observance, which corresponds so strikingly with the Jewish Feast of Tabernacles that, together with other customs, it has led many to believe the Indian nations the descendants of the lost ten tribes of Israel, made it a season of general joy and festivity. All occupations were suspended to give place to social enjoyment in the open air or in arbours formed of the green branches of the trees. Every one appeared in gala dress.

That of the little adopted child consisted of a petticoat of blue broadcloth, bordered with gay-coloured ribbons, and a sack or upper garment of black silk, ornamented with three rows of silver brooches, the centre ones from the throat to the hem being large, while those from the shoulders down were as small as a shilling piece and as closely set as possible. Around her neck were innumerable strings of white and purple *wampum*—an Indian ornament manufactured from the inner surface of the mussel shell. Her hair was clubbed behind and loaded with beads of various colours, while leggings of scarlet cloth and moccasins of deerskin embroidered with porcupine quills completed her costume.

Colonel Johnson was received with all the consideration due his position and the long friendship that existed between him and the tribe.

Observing that the hilarity of the festival had warmed and opened all hearts, the colonel took occasion in an interview with the chief to expatiate upon the parental affection which had led the father and mother of little Eleanor to give up friends and home and come hundreds of miles, in the single hope of looking upon their child and embracing her. The heart of the chief softened as he listened to this recital, and he was induced to promise that he would attend the Grand Council soon to be held at Fort Niagara, on the British side of the river, and bring his little sister with him.

He exacted a promise from Colonel Johnson, however, that not only should no effort be made to reclaim the child, but that even no proposition to part with her should be made to him.

The time at length arrived when, her heart bounding with joy, little Nelly was placed on horseback to accompany her Indian brother to the Great Council of the Senecas. She had promised him that she would never leave him without his permission, and he relied confidently on her word.

How anxiously the hearts of the parents beat with alternate hope and fear as the chiefs and warriors arrived in successive bands to meet their Father, the agent, at the Council Fire! The officers of the fort had kindly given them quarters for the time being, and the ladies, whose sympathies were strongly excited, had accompanied the mother to the place of council and joined in her longing watch for the first appearance of the band from the Allegheny River.

At length the Indians were discerned emerging from the forest on the opposite or American side. Boats were sent by the commanding officer to bring the chief and his party across. The father and mother, attended by all the officers and ladies, stood upon the grassy bank awaiting their approach. They had seen at a glance that the Indians had the little captive with them.

As he was about to enter the boat, the chief said to some of his young men, "Stand here with the horses and wait until I return."

He was told that the horses would be ferried across and taken care of.

"No," said he; "let them wait."

He held little Eleanor by the hand until the river was crossed, until the boat touched the bank, until the child sprang forward into the arms of the mother from whom she had so long been separated.

Witnessing that outburst of affection, the chief could resist no longer.

"She shall go," said he. "The mother must have her child again. I will go back alone."

With one silent gesture of farewell he turned and stepped on board the boat. No arguments or entreaties could induce him to remain at the council. Reaching the other side of the Niagara, he mounted his horse, and with his young men was soon lost in the depths of the forest.

After a few weeks' sojourn at Niagara, Mr. Lytle, dreading lest the resolution of the Big White Man should be shaken, and he should once more be deprived of his child, determined again to change his place of abode. Accordingly, he took the first opportunity of crossing Lake Erie with his family, and settled in the neighbourhood of Detroit, where he afterwards continued to reside.

Little Nelly saw her friend the chief no more. But she never forgot him. To the day of her death she remembered with tenderness and gratitude her brother the Big White Man, and her friends and playfellows among the Senecas.

The Story of Old Fort Dearborn
(Extract)

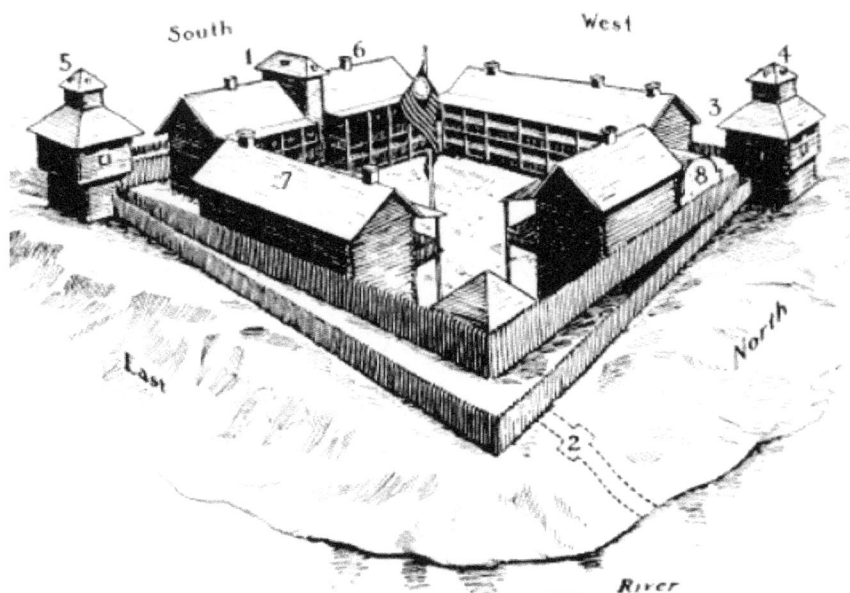

BIRDSEYE VIEW OF OLD FORT DEARBORN

1. Main entrance of the fort passing beneath a building, the upper storey of which was directly over the passageway.

2. location of the "sally port" or underground passage running from the interior of the fort to the river.

3. Gateway to the west

4. Blockhouse at the northwest corner of the fort.

5. Blockhouse at the southeast corner of the fort.

6. Officers' quarters

7. Barracks for the troops

8. Magazine

Contents

The Tragedy

The echoes of the Napoleonic wars raging throughout Europe during the period before and after our war with Great Britain were heard even in this far-away region of the western frontier. England and her continental allies were engaged in a gigantic struggle with France under Napoleon, then at the height of his power. For the purpose of crippling her adversary England issued, in 1807, her famous Orders in Council, which declared that the vessels of neutral nations were liable to seizure if engaged in trade with the enemy. Napoleon retaliated by issuing the equally famous Decrees of Berlin and Milan, which declared Great Britain to be in a state of blockade, and that all vessels bound to or from British ports were liable to capture.

To enforce the Orders in Council was a comparatively easy task for the English navy, then as now the most powerful among the nations; and in consequence the ocean commerce of the Americans suffered severely, for at that time every ocean highway was thronged with the merchant ships of the United States. The interference with our commerce was greatly aggravated by the high-handed action of the English in forcibly taking away from our ships many of their seamen and pressing them into the service of the English navy. This grievance especially became so exasperating that the war spirit of the American people was aroused from one end of the land to the other.

But the protests of the Americans, though made to both England and France, were disregarded, and it was realized that war could not be avoided with one or the other of those nations. Indeed, the proposal was frequently made in the press and in Congress that the country ought to declare war against both powers in view of the outrages suffered by our people. Larned says, though:

> The insolence of the powerful belligerents toward the young republic of the United States was hard to endure, the conduct of the French Government was more insulting, if possible, and more injurious, than that of Great Britain.

But the American people, still inspired by the feelings inherited from the Revolutionary strife, seemed more incensed at the treatment they received from the English than from the French.

The sparse settlements of the West and the isolated posts on the frontier were confronted with a more serious and imminent menace to their safety than were the inhabitants of the older portions of the country on the Atlantic seaboard. They beheld the war cloud gathering, with a dreadful apprehension of the certainty that it would bring upon them a sanguinary conflict with the savages of the wilderness.

The increasingly hostile relations between the Americans and the Western tribes, extending over a period of some years previous to the time of which we are writing, was brought to a climax through the disturbing influence of Tecumseh; but at the Battle of Tippecanoe in the fall of 1811, where the savages met with disastrous defeat, it was thought that at length an era of peace on the frontier was about to follow. And this, no doubt, would have been the case had it not been for the activity of British agents along the Canada border.

It soon became manifest that Indian hostility was once more increasing, and it was generally regarded as due to the machinations of the British at Maiden in Canada, where they gave welcome and shelter to the discontented chiefs and their followers who sought their protection. Forays and attacks, sporadic expeditions of the savages for purposes of plunder or the taking of the scalps of settlers, were continually reported throughout the years 1811 and 1812. One of the causes of war recited by President Madison in his message to Congress just previous to the declaration of war against England was the attacks of the savages upon the frontier settlements incited by British traders. The President said:

A warfare which is known to spare neither age nor sex, and distinguished by features peculiarly shocking to humanity.

When at length the Indian tribes became assured that war between the English and the Americans was about to follow, it was readily seen that they would act for their own interests, and that they would be found opposed to the Americans. The sympathies of the tribes were plainly with the English by reason of the fact that the latter were more liberal in making presents to them than the Americans were. Every year the Indians gathered at Maiden, opposite Detroit, to receive presents both useful and ornamental. Besides blankets and pro visions, a large quantity of objects suitable for the adornment of their persons were distributed among them for the purpose, as it was alleged, of "stimulating trade."

Thus the Western Indians passed by the American trading posts at Chicago, St. Joseph and other stations, and travelled over the old Sauk Trail, which extended from the Mississippi at Rock Island around the southern shore of Lake Michigan, loaded with furs, which they sold to the English traders at Maiden. In addition to the goods received in barter by them, they were shown many favours by the English Government officials, and the friendship thus cultivated proved of immense value to the English when war broke out. In that war the Indians were generally found righting on the side of their English friends.

Another cause of the hostility shown by the Indians toward the Americans was the constant irritation created in their minds after treaties had been concluded. These treaties, though formally agreed to by the chiefs representing their tribes, were often regarded by the Indians as without validity for one reason or another. Indeed, the Indians were not without grievances against the Americans, some real and others conjured up and distorted by wrong-headed leaders among them.

Added to this was the difficulty of restraining the squatter and the bushranger, who defied all treaties, trampled upon the rights of the Indians, and disregarded the treaty obligations of the government. The frontiersman had scant consideration for the red man, whom he looked upon as his natural enemy and the principal obstacle to his safety and well-being. This feeling constituted a natural antagonism which was not allayed until the final removal of all the tribes to government reservations many years later.

In the summer of the year 1812 the officers on duty at Fort Dearborn were Captain Nathan Heald, the commanding officer; Lieutenant Linai T. Helm, Ensign George Ronan and Surgeon Isaac van Voorhis. Captain Heald was at that time thirty-seven years old and the other three officers were all well under thirty; Ronan was the youngest of them all, having graduated from West Point only the year before.

The force composing the garrison consisted, according to Captain Heald's own account written a couple of months afterward, of sixty-six enlisted men, fifty-four of whom were regulars, and twelve militia. In addition to these there were nine women and eighteen children. This makes a total, including the officers, of ninety-seven persons. Some accounts, however, give a different enumeration, but we shall make no attempt to reconcile them, as the variations are not many.

The news that the United States had declared war against Great Britain was received at Fort Dearborn on the seventh day of August, 1812. This was fifty days afterwards, and it had taken this long time for the news to reach the remote post on the frontier. The authorities at Detroit, however, had been informed some three or four weeks before the messenger was finally despatched to Fort Dearborn. If word had been sent as soon as received at Detroit, there is no reasonable doubt that timely measures might have been taken to prevent the terrible disaster which followed. The despatches containing this important announcement were brought by a chief of the Potawatami tribe named Winnemeg, also called Winamac, who was friendly to the Americans and sent by General Hull to Captain Heald.

General William Hull, then in command of the Northwestern army assembled at Detroit, had served with distinction in the Revolutionary War, and had rendered excellent service as governor of the Territory during the previous seven years. Until he surrendered Detroit he was held in high esteem and possessed the confidence of the administration.

A letter of instructions to Captain Heald from General Hull was the most important among the despatches brought by the messenger. This letter gave specific directions to the officer commanding at Fort Dearborn, and was as follows:

> It is with regret I order the evacuation of your post, owing to the want of provisions only, a neglect of the Commandant of Detroit. You will therefore destroy all arms and ammunition.; but the goods of the factory you may give to the friendly Indians who may be desirous of escorting you on to Fort Wayne, and to the poor and needy of your post. I am informed this day that Mackinac and the Island of St. Joseph's (in the St. Mary's River) will be evacuated on account of the scarcity of provisions, and I hope in my next to give you an account of the surrender of the British at Maiden, as I expect 600 men here by the beginning of Sept.
>
> [Signed]   Brigadier Gen. Hull.

The letter, the original of which is preserved in the Draper collection of manuscripts at Madison, Wisconsin, bears the marks of having been hastily written. Evidently Mrs. John H. Kinzie, when she wrote the first published accounts of the events here narrated, had never seen the letter in which is contained the order to evacuate. In her work entitled *Wau-Bun* she says that the order received by Captain Heald from General Hull was:

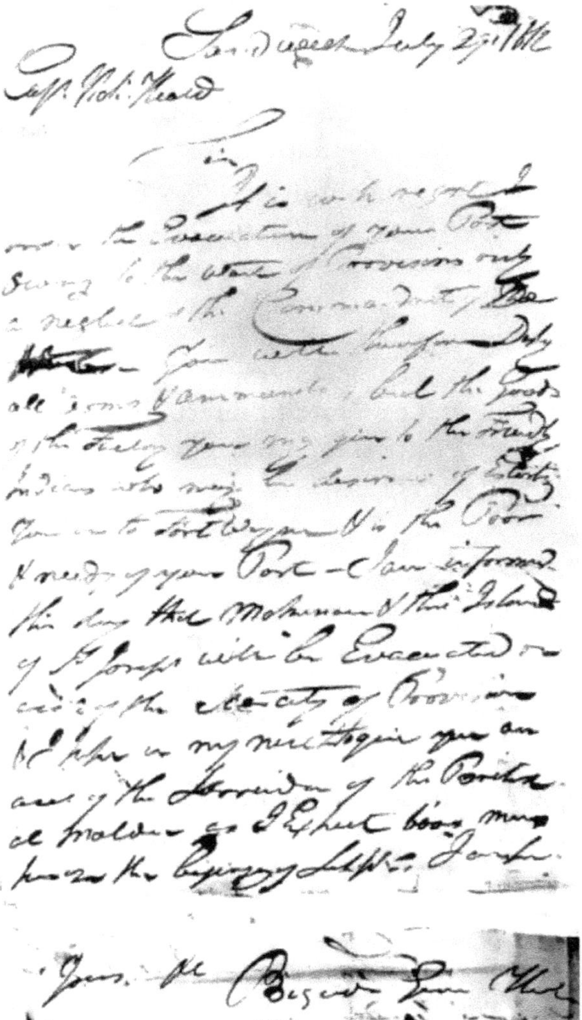

Facsimile of letter of General Hull to Captain Heald

To evacuate the fort, if practicable; and in that event, to distribute all the United States property contained in the fort and in the United States Factory or agency among the Indians in the neighbourhood.

Mrs. Kinzie's account of the order was doubtless gathered from those who were participants in the affairs of that time and who gave the contents of General Hull's letter from memory. For it must be remembered that the author of *Wau-Bun*, in which was printed the first authentic account of these events, was not a participant in them. She was the wife of John H. Kinzie, the son of John Kinzie the pioneer of 1804, and she did not come to Chicago until 1833, twenty-one years after the occurrences of which we are writing.

The original letter has come to light only within the last few years; and upon making a comparison with the *Wau-Bun* account it is seen that General Hull ordered the evacuation, without leaving anything whatever to the discretion of the officer to whom the order is addressed, though discretionary permission is implied by the conditional clause "if practicable" in the *Wau-Bun* account. Just how far Captain Heald would have been justified in using his discretion and disregarding the order to evacuate in view of the great danger there was in obeying it, is a question upon which there were opposing views then, and regarding which there has since been much controversy. It is plain, however, that a strict construction of the order would have required that the post be evacuated, no matter how serious the consequences of doing so might be; and judging from what we know of Captain Heald's character, it is not at all strange that he interpreted his orders literally.

The difficulties with which Captain Heald was encompassed can be but dimly realized. Far removed, as he was, from the nearest post; surrounded by hordes of savages who, though professing friendship, were without doubt in sympathy with the enemy, he well knew that whatever course he might adopt would endanger the safety of the people under his care. His orders to evacuate were indeed positive; but if he could have been assured of safety by remaining and holding the post, he would have been justified without doubt in doing so; and it was the unanimous opinion of his advisers, including the officers of the garrison, that this should be done.

Captain Heald's problem, however, was a military one; he believed in obeying orders, on the theory that his superiors issued them as a part of a comprehensive plan. If he should remain at the post in defiance of his plain instructions he might embarrass a well-planned campaign and invite disaster in a larger field than he could be aware of. Thus, he decided (for though slow in his judgments, he was a man of much decision of character) that the evacuation must be made, and the many appalling risks of a retreat through the wilderness must be hazarded.

After his arrival with the despatches, the friendly Winnemeg sought out and conferred with John Kinzie, in whom the Indians generally placed much confidence. Kinzie was widely known as "the Indians friend," and the regard felt by the savages of the neighbourhood toward him and his family had heretofore been a powerful influence in protecting the post from their attacks. As it was, many of the young men of the tribes could scarcely be restrained in their desire to in augurate hostilities in spite of their older men, who not only entertained a high regard for Kinzie and his family, but who also realized that the friendship of the Americans was of more value to them than that of the British. Mr. Kinzie had taken up his residence at the fort and was soon in possession of all the material facts contained in Winnemeg's despatches.

Winnemeg, well knowing the temper of the tribes, advised Mr. Kinzie that it would be dangerous to evacuate the post and attempt to pass through a country infested with hostile Indians. The garrison, he said, was well supplied with provisions and means of defence, and the post could withstand a siege until reinforcements arrived. But should Captain Heald decide upon abandoning the post according to his instructions, it ought to be done immediately by all means, before the tribes had become aware of the actual condition of affairs.

All this was promptly communicated to the commandant, but it had little effect upon him, and he expressed his determination to carry out his instructions to the letter, distribute the supplies to the friendly Indians, and evacuate the post. Mr. Kinzie strongly reinforced the advice given by Winnemeg, but without effect, and on the following morning the order received from General Hull was read to the troops on parade.

Five days after the receipt of General Hull's order Captain Heald called a council of the Indians, who were then assembled in considerable numbers in the vicinity of the fort, to acquaint them with his intentions and request of them an escort for the garrison on its march to Fort Wayne.

Rumours of the state of affairs at the fort had already been spread among the Indians, and there were evidences of considerable excitement in their actions and conduct. Some of the savages entered the fort in defiance of the guards and making their way to the officers quarters strode rudely around the living apartments. On one occasion an Indian went into the parlour of the commanding officer and, seizing a rifle, fired it, as an expression of defiance—so it was thought, though some believed it was the signal for an attack. the *Wau-Bun* account says:

> The old chiefs passed backwards and forwards among the assembled groups with the appearance of the most lively agitation, while the squaws rushed to and fro in great excitement, and evidently prepared for some fearful scene.

Notwithstanding these demonstrations, the commanding officer, in a perhaps mistaken endeavour to avoid any appearance of fear or hesitation, attended the council which he had called, though warned against doing so. This council was held on the esplanade adjoining the fort. He was accompanied only by Mr. Kinzie, the officers declining to participate. The officers had been secretly informed, they asserted, that the young men of the tribes in tended to fall upon them when they attended the council and treacherously murder them, but Captain Heald was not convinced that there was any truth in the information.

JOHN H. KINZIE

JULIETTE A. KINZIE

MR AND MRS JOHN H. KINZIE

After the two passed out of the fort gates, the portholes of the blockhouses were opened and the cannons were pointed so as to command the whole assembly. This precaution no doubt saved the lives of the two white men who attended the council. Captain Heald in formed the assembled Indians that he proposed to evacuate the fort, but before doing so it was his intention:

To distribute among them, the next day, not only the goods lodged in the United States Factory, but also the ammunition and provisions, with which the garrison was well supplied.

Following this statement he asked the Potawatamis to furnish him an escort for his troops on their march to Fort Wayne, promising that a liberal reward would be paid to them on their arrival, in addition to the presents he was then about to distribute. This proposal, apparently, was well received, and, "with many professions of friendship and good will, the savages assented to all he proposed, and promised all he required."

But Mr. Kinzie, well knowing the disposition of the Indians, did not place reliance upon the assurance they had given. After the council he had an interview with Captain Heald and earnestly tried to convince him of the utter worthlessness of the promises made by the Indians. He reminded him of the many instances of hostility shown by them during the past year, especially by the Wabash Indians, with whom the Potawatamis were closely associated; and that it had become the settled policy of the Americans to withhold from the savages whatever would aid them in carrying on warfare against the scattered white inhabitants of the frontier; and that the distributions he was now making would directly assist them in their bloody purposes.

Owing to the representations thus made, Captain Heald at length became convinced that it would be dangerous to place in the hands of those who might at any moment become enemies the ammunition he had intended giving to them, and he determined to destroy all except what was necessary for the use of his own troops.

A letter written by Lieutenant Helm some two years afterwards has recently come to light. In this letter is given the amount of supplies and war material at the fort when the order to evacuate was received. Helm says:

> We had two hundred stand of arms, four pieces of artillery, six thousand pounds of powder, and a sufficient quantity of shot, lead, etc. There was a supply of Indian corn and provisions to last three months, exclusive of a herd of two hundred head of horned cattle, and twenty-seven barrels of salt.

The next day after the council was held, the thirteenth, there was a general distribution of blankets, broadcloths, calicoes, paints, etc., among the Indians of the neighbourhood; but in the evening the ammunition was thrown into a well and the liquors emptied into the river. The Indians, who were particularly eager for the ammunition and the liquors, had observed that neither of these articles was forthcoming in the distribution of the day, and under cover of darkness crept as near to the fort as possible in order to ascertain if any attempt was being made to destroy them, as they strongly suspected there would be.

A guard had been placed, however, so that the Indians could not approach close to the scene. But though the prowling savages may not have actually witnessed the proceedings, the work of destruction was accomplished. The Indians were well convinced that all this had been done, especially as the river was so impregnated with the liquors that its waters had the taste of strong grog for some time after ward. All the weapons of warfare not necessary for the use of the soldiers were broken up and thrown into the well, along with quantities of powder, shot, flints and gun-screws.

The eight days intervening between the arrival of the order to evacuate the fort and the actual departure of the garrison were filled with forebodings and anxiety. The inmates of the fort, which now included not only the garrison but the civilian inhabitants of the neighbourhood as well, believed that an

REBEKAH WELLS HEALD

CAPTAIN WILLIAM WELLS

appalling fate—death at the hands of a savage foe—inevitably awaited them. The one exception was Captain Heald, who still had faith that the Indians would be true to their promise and furnish an escort on the " march through." He was convinced that he had succeeded in creating an amicable feeling among the savages, and that the safely of all was assured. The officers of the garrison, finding that Captain Heald failed to call a council with them and that he had expressed an intention of abandoning the fort and proceeding to Fort Wayne with an Indian escort, drew up and presented a remonstrance to him in which it was recited that it was highly improbable that the command would be per-mitted to pass through the country in safety to Fort Wayne. For although it had been said that some of the chiefs had opposed an attack upon the fort, planned the preceding autumn, yet it was well known that they had been actuated in that matter by mo-tives of private regard to one family, that of Mr. Kinzie, and not to any general friendly feeling toward the Americans; and that at any rate it was hardly to be expected that these few individuals would be able to control the whole tribe, who were thirsting for blood.

In another clause of the remonstrance it was added that the march of the troops must be necessarily slow, as their movements must be accommodated to the helplessness of the women and children, of whom there were a number with the detachment; and that their unanimous advice was to remain where they were and fortify themselves as strongly as possible.

The reply made by Captain Heald to the remonstrance was that his force was totally in adequate to an engagement with the Indians;—that is, in withstanding a siege;—that he should unquestionably be censured for remaining when there appeared a prospect of a safe march through; that, upon the whole, he deemed it expedient to assemble the Indians, distribute the property among them, and then ask of them an escort to Fort Wayne, with the promise of a considerable reward upon their safe arrival;—and that he had "full confidence in the friendly professions of the Indians."

The gathering perils that now environed the fort and its inmates were rapidly approaching a climax. A fatal mistake had been made in disregarding Winnemeg's advice to begin the retreat without delay if that course was determined upon. Winnemeg had advised that in such an event everything about the fort should be left standing as it was, and while the Indians were engaged in plundering the abandoned fort the troops might be well on their way to Fort Wayne, and perhaps escape attack altogether. John Kinzie likewise strongly urged the necessity of prompt action if the movement was to be made at all.

The officers held aloof from Captain Heald after the distribution of the supplies had taken place, convinced at length that further efforts to dissuade him from his course were useless. They denounced his purpose as "little short of madness." There were many evidences of insubordination observed among the soldiers, and an atmosphere of gloom pervaded the minds of all in the fort.

On the fourteenth, the day before that decided upon for the evacuation, the general despondency was relieved by the arrival of Captain William Wells from Fort Wayne at the head of a band of about thirty friendly Indians of the Miami tribe mounted on ponies. Captain Wells will always be classed among the heroic figures of the time. He was then in the prime of life, a man about forty years of age, and known throughout the frontier as a "perfect master of everything pertaining to Indian life both in peace and war, and withal a stranger to personal fear."

When General Hull had sent the order to Captain Heald to evacuate his post, he also sent an express to Major B. F. Stickney, Indian agent at Fort Wayne, advising him of the order and requesting him to render to Captain Heald all the information and assistance in his power to give. In accordance with this request, Major Stickney had promptly despatched Captain Wells with a party of Miami warriors. A warm attachment existed between Wells and Heald, and upon the arrival of Wells with his Miamis he was hailed with joy, and the hopes of the people at the fort were revived.

It was Wells's intention to prevent if possible the abandonment of the fort, aware as he was of the hostility of the Potawatamis, for he knew that certain destruction awaited the garrison if it should make the attempt. Possessing a perfect knowledge of the character and disposition of the Indians, derived from his long residence among them, Wells foresaw that the savages would take quick advantage of the whites should they leave the shelter of the fort walls and expose themselves in the open on their long slow march of a hundred and fifty miles to Fort Wayne.

When Wells reached the fort he found to his dismay that most of the ammunition had been destroyed, and that the provisions, blankets and other goods in the factory had been distributed to the Indians. He perceived at once that the means of defence having been so seriously reduced there was now no other course to pursue, and that the march must be attempted.

During the day another council with the Indians was held, and on this occasion the savages were found to be in an angry mood. They immediately reminded the commanding officer that they were aware of the destruction of the ammunition and the liquors and that they regarded it as an act of bad faith. It was with the utmost difficulty that the chiefs could restrain the young men of the tribe from carrying out their sanguinary designs at once. For although there were several of the chiefs who shared the generally hostile feeling of the tribe toward the whites, yet they entertained a regard for the men of the garrison and the traders of the neighbourhood.

The evening of the last day at the fort, Black Partridge, a prominent chief of the Potawatamis, of whom further mention will be made, came to the officers quarters and addressed Captain Heald as follows:

Father, I come to deliver up to you the medal I wear. It was given me by the Americans, and I have long worn it in token of our mutual friendship. But our young men are resolved to imbrue their hands in the blood of the whites. I cannot restrain them, and I will not wear a token of peace while I am compelled to act as an enemy.

The language of this speech cannot, of course, be accepted as the *verbatim* utterance of Black Partridge. He spoke in his own tongue, and the speech was translated by the interpreter, who at that time was John Kinzie. The utterance has, however, become a classic in all the historical accounts pertaining to the events of that time.

An observer taking a survey from the walls of the fort at this time would have beheld the river to the north flowing in a sluggish current toward the lake, then bending to the south until it reached its mouth over a shallow bottom nearly opposite the present Madison Street. On the bank of the river, near its mouth, stood the house of Charles Lee, the owner of "Lee's Place," the farm some four miles up the South Branch where two men were murdered by the Indians in the previous April. Toward the west was the Agency House, standing near the bank of the river, beyond which were the groups of Indian *wigwams* clustered along the creek that formerly flowed into the main stream at the present State Street. Opposite this point, on the north bank, was the house of John Burns; and further eastward was the most pretentious residence of the place, the house of John Kinzie. A little in the rear of it stood the cabin of Antoine Ouilmette.

Taking a more distant view toward the west, the observer might have seen the point where the North and South branches of the river met and formed the main body of the stream. The north banks of the river were wooded to the water's edge except where clearings had been made around the cabins mentioned.

Looking eastward, the broad expanse of Lake Michigan stretched away beyond the limits of vision. At the season of year in which the events of which we are writing took place the lake was usually devoid of storms and rough weather.

Lake Michigan at this point has a breadth of fifty miles between the mouth of the Chicago River and the opposite or Michigan shore; and there being no eminence of sufficient height to rise above the horizon, the prospect was like looking off to sea where there is an offing of thousands of miles.

Northward the shores were fringed with a white oak forest,

111

with a line of sand-hills near the beach. Looking southward, the shore of the lake trended away in a curve toward the southeast, and on its margin could be traced the sand-hills characteristic of the shores as far as the eye could reach.

It is a remarkable fact that most of the details of the Chicago massacre are derived from the accounts furnished by the two women who were eyewitnesses of the scenes described. Neither of these accounts was directly written by the two women referred to, but are preserved through secondary reports.

The narrative of Mrs. Helm, who was only seventeen years old at the time, was taken down from dictation apparently by Mrs. John H. Kinzie and incorporated in *Wau-Bun*. While this account, as given in the work mentioned, is enclosed in quotation-marks as if in the language of the narrator, it was evidently rendered by Mrs. Kinzie in her own words. Mrs. Kinzie was not present at the massacre, not having come to Chicago until twenty years thereafter, but she was diligent in procuring all the information available at the time of writing her book. In her later years she no doubt talked the matter over at length with Mrs. Helm, who was a half-sister of her husband.

It is important, in obtaining a clear understanding of this narrative, that the names of Mrs. John Kinzie, the wife of the pioneer of 1804, and of Mrs. John H. Kinzie, the author, be not confused.

The narrative of Mrs. Heald reaches posterity through the story of her son, Darius Heald. A portion was given in John Wentworth's address at the unveiling of the memorial tablet on the site of old Fort Dearborn, delivered May 21, 1881; and another portion is quoted in Joseph Kirkland's book, *The Chicago Massacre*, published some years later.

Darius Heald was not born until ten years after the massacre, and his testimony, written from his dictation, was derived entirely from the oral account of his mother.

Comparing the account with that given by Mrs. Helm a number of discrepancies in details is observed, though the main events are related in both accounts in practically identical form.

The accounts of both Mrs. Helm and Mrs. Heald were written from dictation. Mrs. Helm's account appeared in print twenty-four years after the event which it describes, while Mrs. Heald's did not appear until seventy-five years thereafter, having in the meantime been preserved only in the form of a family tradition. It can therefore hardly have as much historical value as the older published narrative of Mrs. Helm.

The morning of the fifteenth of August, 1812, dawned clear and the day was oppressively warm. There was scarcely a breath of air stirring and the surface of the lake was unruffled, stretching away, as one expressed it, " like a sheet of burnished gold." The preparations for the departure went actively forward. At nine o clock Captain Wells took a place at the head of the column on horseback, his face blackened, according to the Indian custom, "in token of his impending fate." Wells was under no illusions. He knew that at any moment the crisis would be upon them, and he clearly realized how hopeless in the presence of hordes of savages in the neighbourhood, bent on blood and plunder, any resistance would be, and how faint a chance there was for escape. But brave and resolute he calmly went forward with the fixed purpose of doing his duty in the face of inevitable destruction.

Following him rode half of his Miami band, and behind them the musicians came, and as the march began they played the *Dead March*. Then came the soldiers, each carrying twenty-five rounds of ammunition, all that had been reserved from the general destruction, though a totally inadequate supply for such a campaign as they might reasonably look forward to in these threatening circum stances.

Next came a train of wagons in which the camp equipage and provisions were carried, and in the wagons were also placed the women and children. The rear of the column was brought up by the remainder of the Miami escort. The wives of the married officers, Mrs. Heald and Mrs. Helm, accompanied the procession on horseback.

The escort promised by the Potawatamis in council was on hand and moved with the procession, a few hundred yards to the west, keeping a parallel course. There was a lingering hope among the whites that the Indians would be true to their promise and continue with them throughout their journey as a protecting force, and in this hope the movements of the Indians were watched with the greatest interest, though with painful forebodings and suspicions.

Among the people thus hoping against hope:

> There were not wanting gallant hearts who strove to encourage in their desponding companions the hopes of escape they were far from indulging themselves.

Early in the morning of the day of the departure of the garrison John Kinzie had received a message from Topenebe of St. Joseph's band informing him of what he already was well convinced of, that the Potawatamis who were to act as escort on the march had treacherous designs, and would without doubt attack the column. Topenebe was a chief in the Potawatami tribe, but a firm friend of the whites and especially of the Kinzie family. He warned Mr. Kinzie not to accompany the troops when they left the fort, but rather to take passage in a boat with his family and proceed directly to St. Joseph, where he might rejoin the troops if they were successful in passing through the country.

Mr. Kinzie, however, decided to place his family in the boat, while he himself accompanied the troops, in the hope and belief that his presence would operate as a restraint upon the fury of the savages in case of an attack. This brave action on the part of Mr. Kinzie, who thus cast in his lot with those who were going forth to almost certain destruction, must be regarded as an exhibition of rare personal courage notable even among many other instances of a similar kind seen on that fatal day.

The party in the boat which left the Kinzie house about the same time that the troops marched out of the fort consisted of Mrs. Kinzie and her four children, the eldest of whom by her second marriage was John Harris, then nine years old. The others were: Ellen Marion, six and a half years old; Maria Indiana, four years old, and Robert Allen, two and a half years old. In addition there were Josette La Framboise, a French-Ottawa half-breed, a nurse in the family; Chandonnais, a clerk in the employ of Mr. Kinzie; two servants, a boatman, and the two Indians who had brought the message from Topenebe. This made a party of twelve persons in the boat.

Upon Mrs. Kinzie now devolved the responsibility and direction of the party in the boat, since her husband had chosen to accompany the troops. Proceeding to the mouth of the river, the boat was detained for a time while the party beheld the passage of the column just beginning its march. The author of *Wau-Bun* says Mrs. Kinzie:

> Was a woman of uncommon energy and strength of character, yet her heart died within her as she folded her arms around her helpless infants, and gazed upon the march of her husband and eldest child to certain destruction.

It will be recalled that Mrs. Kinzie's eldest child was Mrs. Margaret Helm, who was with her husband on the march.

Antoine Ouilmette and his family did not abandon their dwelling as did all the other residents of the village. A sister of his wife, known in the accounts as Mrs. Bisson, was a member of this same household. Ouilmette was regarded by the Potawatamis as belonging to their tribe, and he felt no apprehension of danger in remaining on the ground. Renegade whites living among the savages usually maintained their standing among them by offering no opposition to any atrocities committed by them, and sometimes even participating in the warfare against their own race.

The line of march lay along the shore of the lake toward the south. In the absence of roads through the country at that early period the travelling was difficult for wagons, and the margin of the lake was usually preferred for that kind of locomotion wherever it lay in the desired direction. For a considerable distance toward the southern end of the lake the route of the proposed march would be along the sandy beach, usually firm and smooth near the water's edge.

Boat navigation was the main reliance for transporting men and goods, though as yet there was not a sufficiently large number of boats of any description on Lake Michigan to have moved so large a body of men and women at one time as composed the procession leaving the fort. And even if there had been enough of such as were used by the traders, it is not likely that the people would have been permitted by the hostile Indians even to embark in them.

The fort was no sooner vacated than the Indians rushed in and began to plunder the place of everything that was movable. In an adjoining field there had been a herd of cattle kept for the use of soldiers, such as milch cows, oxen, etc., and these were allowed to run at large when the troops departed. The Indians gave chase and shot them all, seemingly for the satisfaction they found in the mere act of killing, and the deed was quite in keeping with their usual improvident habits. Mrs. Helm, in her account, said that she well remembered a remark of Ensign Ronan as the shooting of the cattle went on. "Such," said he, " is to be our fate,—to be shot down like beasts."

In taking their departure from the fort there was little in the conduct of the savages to indicate the hostility which was so soon to manifest itself. Mrs. Heald gave an account of the scene many years later, and she said in her narrative that " the fort was vacated quietly, not a cross word being passed between soldiers and Indians, and goodbyes were exchanged."

In fact, it was generally believed that those Indians who gathered about the entrance of the fort, prepared to rush in the moment the last men passed out, took no part in the later events of the day, being fully occupied in their work of plundering and cattle-killing. John Wentworth in one of his lectures on the subject went further, and declared that the Indians who had lived a long time in the immediate vicinity of the fort were friendly to the whites and "did their best to pacify the numerous warriors who flocked here from the more distant hunting grounds."

The column had not proceeded very far on its course before it was noticed that the Potawatami escort was diverging from the direction in which both columns started out and that at the distance of a mile from the fort there was a considerable distance between them.

A range of sand-hills and sand-banks of no great height skirted the shore dividing the sandy beach from the prairie beyond them. Among these sand-hills were a few trees and bushes supporting a precarious existence. Westward of this range of sand-hills which began to rise about a mile from the fort the Indians continued their course and were soon lost to view.

Suddenly, far in the advance, Captain Wells was seen to turn his horse and ride furiously back along the marching men, who quickly came to a halt. Wells was swinging his hat in a circle around his head, which meant in the sign language of the frontier, "We are surrounded by Indians!" As he approached the commanding officer he shouted, "They are about to attack us; form instantly and charge upon them." The Potawatami escort had in fact become the attacking party, choosing to murder the whites rather than join in looting the fort

The Indians could now be seen in great numbers coming into view from "behind the mounds of sand, their heads bobbing up and down "like turtles out of the water." The troops were promptly formed and they had no sooner taken position than the Indians began firing upon them with deadly effect, the first victim being a veteran of seventy years of age.

After firing one round the troops charged up the slopes of the sand-hills, driving the Indians from the position. However, they scattered in both directions and presently began to envelop the flanks of the line according to the usual practice in savage warfare. At this juncture the mounted Miamis would have been of the greatest service in preventing such a manoeuvre, but they had all fled across the prairie after the first shot was fired, quickly disappeared in the distance, and were seen no more.

Captain Heald, in a letter written a few weeks after the event, said:

The situation of the country rendered it necessary for us to take the beach, with the lake on our left, and a high sand-bank on our right, at about one hundred yards distance. We had proceeded about a mile and a half when it was discovered that the Indians were prepared to attack us from behind the bank. I immediately marched up with the company to the top of the bank when the action commenced; after firing one round we charged, and the Indians gave way in front and joined those on our flanks.

The horses upon which Mrs. Heald and Mrs. Helm were riding became almost un manageable after the firing had begun. The explosion of a charge in an old flint lock musket was a terrific outburst of noise. It produced a volume of sound which we can scarcely realize when comparing it with the report of a service rifle in use at the present day. It was little wonder that the horses pranced and bounded when these thundering volleys were heard.

Mrs. Helm said that she drew off a little and gazing upon her husband (Lieutenant Helm) and her father (Mr. Kinzie), whom, although he was her stepfather, she was always fond of calling father, she saw that they both were yet unharmed. But she felt that as for herself her hour had come, and she endeavoured to forget those she loved, and to prepare herself for her approaching fate.

It was the endeavour of the savages to close upon their victims whenever they found an opportunity to bring their tomahawks and scalping knives into use. While some were firing upon the troops from cover, others were seeking to attack those who had become separated from their friends. These they could quickly overcome owing to their skill in the use of those murderous weapons.

One Sergeant Holt, who was accompanied by his wife, had received a ball in his neck in the early part of the engagement. He handed his sword to his wife, who was on horseback near him, and told her to defend herself. The Indians were desirous of obtaining possession of the horse and at the same time sparing her life, for generally they wished to take the women captives. Mrs. Holt resisted vigorously when the savages at tempted to seize the horse; she broke away from them and dashed out

on the open prairie. Still pursuing, they overtook her and succeeded in dragging her from her horse. She was then made a
prisoner and later taken to the Illinois River country, where
she received kind treatment. Ultimately she was ransomed and
restored to her friends.

Mrs. Helm was attacked by a young Indian, who raised his
tomahawk, intending to deal her a blow, but she avoided the
murderous weapon and seized her assailant around the neck.
This is the moment that the sculptor of the bronze group, now
situated at the intersection of Eighteenth Street and Calumet
Avenue, chose for his representation. Mrs. Helm tried to get
possession of the scalping knife which hung in a scabbard over
his breast, but another and an older Indian dragged her away
with a strong grasp. Struggling and resisting, she was then borne
toward the lake, plunged into the water and firmly held, as if it
were the intention to drown her. She soon perceived, however,
that the object of her captor was not to drown her, as he held
her in such a position as to keep her head above water. She began to gather courage, and looking the savage full in the face,
she saw at once, notwithstanding the paint with which he had
disguised himself, that it was Black Partridge, the chief who had
surrendered his medal to the commandant the evening before.

When the firing was nearly over, the chief brought her out of
the water and placed her on a sand-bank. She said:

It was a burning August morning, and walking through
the sand in my drenched condition was inexpressibly
painful and fatiguing. I stooped and took off my shoes
to free them from the sand with which they were nearly
filled, when a squaw seized them and carried them off,
and I was obliged to proceed without them.

As she gained the prairie she was met by Mr. Kinzie, who
informed her that her husband (Lieutenant Helm) was safe, and
but slightly wounded. She was led back to the Indian encampment on the banks of the Chicago River. She continues in her
story:

At one time I was placed upon a horse without a saddle, but finding the motion insupportable, I sprang off. Supported partly by my kind conductor, Black Partridge, and partly by another Indian, Pee-so-tum, who held dangling in his hand a scalp, which by the black ribbon around the queue I recognized as that of Captain Wells, I dragged my fainting steps to one of the *wigwams*.

Arrived at the entrance of a chief's *wigwam*, the wife of the chief, inspired by a sentiment of pity for her, an exhibition of feeling rare among Indian women, seeing her exhausted condition, took a kettle and, dipping up some water from the small creek nearby, threw in a quantity of maple sugar, and, stirring it with her hand, gave the mixture to her to drink. She was greatly refreshed by the draught. This act of kindness touched the poor young woman deeply, occurring as it did in the midst of so many horrors.

In the meantime the men in the ranks fell rapidly under the withering fire of their savage foes, who were now on all sides of them in overwhelming numbers. Still they continued the struggle bravely, and the prairie was soon thickly scattered with dead and wounded. Captain Heald himself received a wound in his hip, from which he suffered for the remainder of his life, and which caused his death some years later. It may be stated in passing that the bodies of those who were killed in this bloody combat lay exposed to the elements and wild beasts for four years, until eventually their remains were gathered up and buried by United States soldiers arriving to rebuild the fort.

The troops behaved most gallantly while the battle lasted and seemed determined to make as brave a defence as possible. They were soon reduced to about one-half of their original number. After the action had continued about a quarter of an hour Captain Heald drew off the few men still remaining and took possession of a small elevation in the open prairie, beyond the range of the shots coming from the sand-hills which the Indians now held, thus having reversed the positions which the opposing forces occupied at the beginning of the battle.

There was nothing now to prevent the savages from attacking the wagons containing the women and children. The troops were isolated on the prairie and could not even defend themselves, much less could they do anything to protect the helpless people in the wagons.

Meantime Captain Wells was fighting, Indian fashion, and doing more execution than any other man on the field. Mounted on horseback, he freely exposed himself wherever the combat was most furious. He was armed with a rifle and carried two pistols. His powder and bullets were carried in belts slung over his shoulders, convenient for instant use. He usually had the bullet needed for the next load ready in his mouth. " He would pour in the powder," said an eyewitness, "wad it down, blow in the bullet, prime, and fire, more rapidly than one can tell the facts."

The savages had a wholesome fear of Wells, and they fled from his aim in all directions. They broke from him right and left. In the effort to protect the women and children he closely watched the movements of the Indians toward the wagons, and presently saw a young savage come up and enter one of them in which twelve of the children had been collected. Before he could prevent him, the savage ruthlessly tomahawked the entire group; and when Wells caught sight of this horrid deed, he shouted in rage: "Is that their game—butchering women and children?"

But his own end was near. He received a shot which passed through his lungs, and realising that it was a mortal wound, he rode up to his niece, Mrs. Heald, still maintaining his position upon his horse. Seizing her hand, he exclaimed, " Farewell, my child."

Mrs. Heald, who, though thus addressed, was nearly as old as her uncle, replied, "Why, uncle, I hope you will get over this."

"No, my child," he said, "I cannot." She then saw that blood was coming from his nose and mouth, and he said that he could not last five minutes longer. He then gave his niece his last message in these words: "Tell my wife, if you live to get there,—but

I think it doubtful if a single one gets there,—tell her I died at my post doing the best I could. There are seven red devils over there that I have killed."

Wells's horse had already been shot through the body, and at that moment fell exhausted, with his rider pinioned beneath him. Wells then saw several Indians coming toward him, bent on taking advantage of his apparent helplessness. He summoned his failing strength and from his prostrate position took aim and killed one of them on the spot. The others approached closer to the wounded lion, determined to strike a blow or fire a shot that would instantly end his life. Mrs. Heald saw the movement and cried out, "Uncle, there is an Indian pointing right at the back of your head." He put his hand back and held up his head, in spite of his failing strength, so that better aim might be taken, and then exclaimed, "Shoot away!"

The Indian fired and Captain Wells fell dead. Thus perished the man to whom in a greater degree than to any other person those who still remained alive upon the scene looked for help and guidance in this awful extremity. Without him, the thickening perils of the hour seemed the climax of despair.

Sometime later the news of the death of Captain Wells reached his widow (the daughter of the chief Little Turtle), long before Mrs. Heald, who survived the massacre, was able to convey the message entrusted to her. One of the Indians present who witnessed the scene, though he took no part in the perpetration of that dark deed, was a friend of Wells, whom he had known in former years and whom he regarded as a brother. It was this Indian who went to Fort Wayne after the battle was over and gave Mrs. Wells the first intimation of her husband's death. After doing so he disappeared, and it was supposed that he returned to his tribe, as he was not seen again.

The two younger officers, Ensign George Ronan and Surgeon Isaac Van Voorhis, had been all this time gallantly bearing their part in the unequal struggle with the savage hordes that surrounded them, and both of them had received dangerous wounds. In her account of the battle, Mrs. Helm says that, overwrought by his fighting and pain, the surgeon came up and addressed her. He had been wounded, his horse had been shot under him, and he was in a state of terror. Aware of Mrs. Helm's lifelong experience with the Indians, though she was much younger than himself, he said to her: "Do you think they will take our lives? I am badly wounded, but I think not mortally. Perhaps we might purchase our lives by promising them a large reward. Do you think there is any chance?"

"Dr. Van Voorhis," said the seventeen-year-old girl, "do not let us waste the few moments that yet remain to us in such vain hopes. Our fate is inevitable. In a few moments we must appear before the bar of God. Let us make what preparation is yet in our power."

"Oh, I cannot die!" he exclaimed. "I am not fit to die. If I had but a short time to prepare! Death is awful!" Mrs. Helm pointed to Ensign Ronan, who, though even then mortally wounded, was down on one knee and was still fighting with desperate courage.

"Look at that man," she said. "At least he dies like a soldier."

"Yes," replied the surgeon, "but he has no terrors of the future—he is an unbeliever!"

The wounded surgeon's fear, thus shown under these trying circumstances, was entirely natural. He was then only twenty-two years of age and had entered the service on the frontier but the year before. The bravest men have often passed through a similar experience in moments of danger. An unbeliever, in his view, would not concern himself with the hereafter; but he considered that he himself was unfit to appear before the bar of God. What more natural than that this young man's heart should fail him in that supreme moment?

There was no opportunity, however, even had he been able, to show his mettle by a renewed effort to stem the tide of disaster, for almost immediately afterwards he was tomahawked by one of the Indians, and was seen dead on the ground when Mrs. Helm passed that way a little time later as the captive of the chief Black Partridge, on their way to the river.

In an obituary notice, published in *The Political Index*, November 17, 1812, at Newburg, New York, there is the following notice of the unfortunate young surgeon:

Among the slain (at the Fort Dearborn Massacre) was Dr. Isaac Van Voorhis, of Fishkill, surgeon in the army. He was a young man of great merit, and received his early education at the academy in this village. He possessed an enterprising and cultivated mind, and was ardent in the support of the interest and honour of his country.

Ensign George Ronan, who was also only twenty-two, had entered the service on the frontier the previous year. He was a graduate of West Point, with the rank of ensign, corresponding to that of second lieutenant in the modern army regulations. He is always referred to as a brave and enterprising young officer. He won the admiration of all during the months previous to the events here narrated, and especially for the courage and devotion shown by him in the last scene, when he perished on the field of battle.

From his position on the battlefield, Captain Heald saw the Indians making signs to him to approach and consult with them. Heald advanced alone in response to this invitation. Through a half-breed interpreter, Peresh Leclerc, he was asked to surrender to them, the Indians at the same time promising to spare the lives of all the prisoners. A Potawatami chief, named Black Bird, was the spokesman for the Indians. Captain Heald in his report says that after a few moments consideration he concluded it would be most prudent to comply with this request, although he did not put entire confidence in the promise.

In fact, Heald was reduced to extremities, and a parley with the Indians was his only hope. They were surrounded by the savages, Lieutenant Helm was wounded and a prisoner in the hands of the enemy, who indeed had possession of all the horses, wagons, and property of every description, besides having killed or captured all the women and children. He was obliged to make the best terms possible, for though a surrender might be followed by treachery, there was really no other course for him to take.

The surrender was then agreed to and the fighting ceased. The air was filled with the shouts of the savages exulting over their victory, while from the wounded issued moans of pain, and from the distance could be heard the wailings of cruelly bereaved mothers.

After delivering up their arms, the survivors were taken back to the encampment of the Indians near the fort, and distributed among the different tribes. The number of their warriors, Heald said, was between four hundred and five hundred, mostly of the Potawatami nation, and the loss on their side was about fifteen. There were about sixty of the whites killed in the battle and the massacre which followed, but when the troops surrendered and the Indians promised that the lives of the survivors should be spared, it was found that the savages regarded the wounded as exempted from this condition. Accordingly, many of the wounded were ruthlessly tomahawked after the surrender, and in the same evening five of the soldiers were tortured to death. A number of others perished from the privations they suffered while in the hands of the Indians during the ensuing season.

The boat containing the Kinzie family and the servants accompanying them at first kept near the mouth of the river, the occupants watching the troops and the wagon train passing along the beach toward the south. They heard the discharge of the guns when the Indians attacked, and the boat's course was directed so as to approach as nearly as possible to the scene of the fighting. They saw a woman on horseback led by an Indian not far from the edge of the water.

"That is Mrs. Heald," cried Mrs. Kinzie. "That Indian will kill her. Run, Chandonnais, take the mule that is tied there and offer it to him to release her." The Indian was already attempting to take off her bonnet, with the evident intention of scalping her, and she was resisting vigorously.

The Indian paused long enough in the struggle to listen to the offer made by Chandonnais, who added the promise of two bottles of whiskey as soon as they would reach their destination. "But," said the Indian, "she is badly wounded—she will die. Will you give me the whiskey at all events?" Chandonnais, who was well known to the Indians, promised that he would, and the bargain was concluded. Several squaws, keen for plunder, had followed the procession closely, and made an ineffectual attempt to rob Mrs. Heald of her shoes and stockings. The savage had succeeded in getting possession of her bonnet, and placed it on his own head. She was taken on board the boat, and lay moaning with pain from the wounds she had received.

As it was impossible to continue their journey under the circumstances, the boat and its passengers returned to the Kinzie house, trusting to the influence possessed by Mr. Kinzie to maintain their safety. They were joined there by Mr. Kinzie, who had escaped injury from the savages. Around them gathered a number of Indians still friendly to the Kinzie family, whose intentions were to assist them in a renewed attempt to reach their proposed destination at St. Joseph.

Among the friendly Indians thus gathered was Black Partridge, who had rescued Mrs. Helm and had safely brought her to the Kinzie house, where she rejoined her family.

Thus were assembled the entire family of John Kinzie, except his son-in-law, Lieutenant Helm. Mrs. Heald and Mrs. Helm were both suffering from wounds. Both had been attacked by the savages while on horseback, the former having perhaps escaped death, through the ransom negotiated by Chandonnais, and the other having been rescued by Black Partridge.

John Burns, with his wife and infant child, had lived in the house west of the Kinzies', on the north bank of the river, and were with the troops at the time of the attack. It will be recalled that Mrs. Burns and her one-day-old infant had been brought to the fort for safety at the time of the Indian alarm in the previous April. Burns was killed while with the troops, but his wife and child were made captives by one of the chiefs and by him taken to his village and treated with great kindness; but his squaw wife, excited by feelings of jealousy of the favours shown to the captives, attempted to kill the child with a tomahawk thrown at it with great force. The blow narrowly missed being fatal, but it inflicted a wound the marks of which she carried through the remainder of her life. The chief prevented further attempts of the kind by removing the captives to a place of safety. Eventually the mother and child found their way back to civilization. The younger Mrs. Kinzie, writes in *Wau-Bun:*

> Twenty-two years after this, as I was on a journey to Chicago in the steamer *Uncle Sam*, a young woman, hearing my name, introduced herself to me, and raising the hair from her forehead, showed me the mark of the tomahawk which had so nearly been fatal to her."

A somewhat similar case was that of Mrs. Charles Lee, whose husband owned the farm on the South Branch where the two men were murdered by Indians in the previous April. His son, a lad of twelve years, who, with the discharged soldier, ran to the fort from the farm and gave the alarm on that occasion, was also with the troops in company with his father. Lee and his son were both killed in the battle, but Mrs. Lee and her young child were captured, and later came into the possession of Black Partridge. This "knightly rescuer of women" proved the worth of his friendship toward the whites in the case of Mrs. Lee and her child, as he had already done in the rescue of Mrs. Helm.

The story of John Cooper, surgeon's mate at Fort Dearborn, was similar in many of its details to that of others in the battle. Cooper was accompanied by his wife and two young daughters, the elder of whom was named Isabella. Cooper was among the killed, and when the Indians made a rush for the women and children in the wagons, a young Indian boy attempted to carry off Isabella, but encountered so lively a resistance that he was obliged to throw her down. He succeeded in scalping her, and would have killed her outright had not an old squaw prevented him. The squaw, who knew the Cooper family, took Mrs. Cooper and her children to her *wigwam* and cured the girl of her wound.

The family remained in captivity two years, when they were ransomed. They afterwards lived in Detroit. The mark of the wound on the girl's head caused by the young Indian's scalping knife was about the size of a silver dollar, and, of course, remained with her through her life.

An infant of six months was with its mother among the survivors of that dreadful day. Corporal Simmons had with him on the march his wife and two children, the eldest a boy of two years, and a little girl an infant in its mother's arms. The mother and her children were in the army wagon, which was entered by the Indian, who despatched the children as rapidly as he could reach them. Mrs. Simmons, while not able to save her boy, succeeded in concealing the baby in a shawl behind her, and the child survived the scenes of that day. The corporal himself was among those who were slain.

When the division of prisoners took place after the action Mrs. Simmons was carried off by the Indians to Green Bay, the whole distance to which she walked, carrying her child in her arms. On arriving at their destination the captives were required to "run the gauntlet," according to the brutal custom of the savages, but in doing so she was able to protect her precious charge by bending over it as she held it in her arms. She received many cruel blows and half dead she reached the goal where a friendly squaw gave her and her child a kind reception. In the following year, after many weary wanderings, Mrs. Simmons reached a frontier post in Ohio and was at length set at liberty.

This child grew up and became the wife of Moses Winans, and in later life she and her husband lived in California, but she never returned to Chicago again. She died in 1903, at the advanced age of ninety years.

Of the nine women who set out with the troops, two were killed; the others, except Mrs. Heald and Mrs. Helm, were carried off by the savages, and some did not survive the hardships of the life they were compelled to undergo. There were eighteen children, of whom twelve were killed outright, and but few of the others were ever heard of.

The following fall and winter the British, then in posses-sion of Detroit, were urged by some of the American residents of that place to exert their influence among their Indian allies to return the captives to the custody of the British military au-thorities. Tardy efforts were made, and at length the agent who was appointed for that work reported that he had gathered at the St. Joseph River seventeen soldiers, four women, and some children.

There were, however, several other survivors not included among those whom the British agent was able to find, as appears from some other accounts. The soldiers were taken to Detroit and became prisoners of war, but their condition was thus only slightly ameliorated. Young John Kinzie, then a lad ten years of age, recalled that while his father's family were living in their own house at Detroit during that winter, themselves practically prisoners of war, he saw the miserable captives suffering from ex-posure in the severe cold weather without adequate shelter, and but little could be done for them by their American friends.

The perils surrounding the Kinzie family when they were once more gathered under the family roof were of the most serious character. Here were assembled a company of the sur-vivors after a day of excitement, bloodshed, and distress hardly to be paralleled in the lives of civilized people. Across the river from the Kinzie house could be seen the victorious savages in-dulging in wild antics, shouting and dancing exultantly, ransack-ing and plundering the buildings within the fort, and prepar-ing to torture some of the prisoners to death. They had arrayed themselves in women's hats, shawls, and ribbons, and filled the air with their savage outcries.

Notwithstanding the fact that the house and its inmates were closely guarded by their Indian friends, and that Black Partridge and other friendly Indians had established themselves in the porch of the building as sentinels, to protect the family from any evil that the young men of the tribes might endeavour to commit, their peril was extreme. Everything remained tranquil, however, during the day, and the following night was passed in comparative freedom from alarms.

The next day the Indians set fire to the fort and the entire place was consumed. A party of Indians from the Wabash arrived at this time, having heard of the intended evacuation of the fort, and eager to share in the plunder. They were disappointed and enraged on finding that their arrival was too late, that the spoils had been divided, and the scalps all taken. These Indians had no particular regard for the Kinzies, and it at once became evident that their presence boded destruction to the devoted inmates of the house. They blackened their faces and proceeded to the Kinzie house as the most promising spot to carry out their plundering and bloodthirsty designs.

Black Partridge was especially anxious in behalf of Mrs. Helm, whose safety he wished to assure. By his directions she disguised herself and took refuge in the house of Ouilmette. Ouilmette, being a Frenchman, and living with an Indian wife, was never molested by the Indians at any time, being regarded as one of themselves.

The Indians approached this house first and entered without ceremony. Mrs. Bisson, sister of Ouilmette's wife, hastily concealed Mrs. Helm by covering her with a feather bed. She then took her seat in front of the bed and occupied herself with her sewing. The Indians looked into every part of the room, but did not raise the feather mattress under which Mrs. Helm was lying, half smothered. Mrs. Bisson was in terror for her own safety, but bravely maintained an air of indifference during this trying ordeal, and presently the Indians left the house.

They then went over to the Kinzie dwelling, entered the principal room, and seated themselves on the floor in ominous silence. Black Partridge then spoke in a low voice to Waubansee, who was with him as one of the guards, and said: "We have endeavoured to save our friends, but it is in vain—nothing will save them now."

At that moment a friendly whoop, loud and clear, was heard from the bank of the river opposite to the house, and Black Partridge instantly arose and ran toward the landing, calling out,

"Who are you?"

"I am the Sauganash," came the reply.

Black Partridge replied, "Then make all speed to the house; your friend is in danger, and you alone can save him."

Sauganash, also known as Billy Caldwell, was a half-breed and was a chief of the Potawatami tribe, and a man of great influence among the Indians. He was not present at the evacuation and massacre of the day before, but had come in time to save the lives of many of the prisoners. With him had come the chief Shabbona, who also used his influence in moderating the brutality of the younger members of the tribes.

The Sauganash hastened across the river, while the threatening savages waited in wonder for his appearance. He calmly entered the room, stood his rifle behind the door, and gazed about him at the silent savages squatting on the floor. He boldly asked them why they had blackened their faces. "Is it that you are mourning for the friends you have lost in battle?"—thus purposely misunderstanding their evil designs, which he easily penetrated. "Or is it," he continued, "that you are fasting? If so, ask our friend here, and he will give you to eat. He is the Indians friend, and never yet refused them what they had need of."

The savages were taken by surprise at this speech, and none among them had the courage to say what the purpose was in their minds. One of them answered that they had come to ask for some white cotton cloth in which they might wrap the bodies of their dead friends before placing them in their graves. As soon as this was said they were provided with a quantity of cloth, and to the relief of everyone they took their departure peaceably.

Quartermaster Sergeant William Griffith escaped the general massacre by a series of remarkable strokes of good fortune. While the troops were leaving the fort it was discovered that the horses carrying the surgeon's apparatus and medicines had strayed off. Griffith went to search for them and bring them up, but being unsuccessful, he hastened to join the column on foot. Before he had proceeded very far he was met and made a prisoner by the chief Topenebe, who was friendly to the whites. The chief took him to the river and put him in a canoe, paddled it across the river and told him to hide himself in the thick woods on the north side.

The next day he cautiously appeared in the vicinity of Ouilmette's house, and the place seeming to be quiet, he entered the cabin at the rear. This was just after the Wabash Indians had left the house for that of Mr. Kinzie.

The family were greatly alarmed at his appearance, and he was at once stripped of his army uniform; he was arrayed in a suit of deerskin, with belt, *moccasins*, and pipe, like a French *engagé*. His dark complexion and black whiskers favoured the disguise, and all were instructed to address him in French, although he was ignorant of the language. In this character he joined the Kinzie family and with them eventually reached a place of safety.

After the surrender Captain Heald was kept unmolested, quite fortunately being given into the custody of an Indian from the Kankakee, who, it seems, had known him previously, and who had formed an attachment for him. The Indian at once made plans for his escape, and soon Captain Heald was placed in a canoe and taken to St. Joseph. Here he was joined by Mrs. Heald, and they both pursued their journey up the east coast of Lake Michigan to Mackinac, where Captain Heald delivered himself up as a prisoner of war to the British commandant, by whom he was well treated and released on parole. Later in the season he found means to reach Louisville, where Mrs. Heald's father, Colonel Samuel Wells, resided. It had been supposed that both Heald and his wife had perished in the massacre, and their appearance was as if they had awakened from the dead.

In due course of time Heald was exchanged, and again entered the service with the rank of major. He never got rid of the effects of his wound, and in 1817 he resigned his commission in the army and removed with his family to a small town in Missouri, where he died a few years later.

Lieutenant Helm, who was among the wounded at the time of the surrender, had the good fortune to fall into the hands of some friendly Indians, and was taken to Peoria. He was liberated through the intervention of Thomas Forsyth, the half-brother of Mr. Kinzie, who was the Indian agent at that place. Forsyth had great influence with the Potawatamis. Reynolds says:

He had been raised with this nation, spoke their language well, and was well acquainted with their character.

He advanced the amount demanded by the Indians for Helm's ransom, and had him sent to St. Louis in safety. In this important and dangerous service Forsyth risked his life every moment he was engaged in it, for the Indians at that time were in a highly inflamed condition.

Eventually Lieutenant Helm rejoined his wife at Detroit.

The final scene in the story of old Fort Dearborn was the departure of the Kinzie family and their retinue of servants on the third day after the battle and massacre. The fort and the agency house had been destroyed by fire on the second day, and there were now remaining only the Kinzie house, the Ouilmette cabin near it, the house lately occupied by John Burns and his wife and child on the north bank of the main river, and that lately occupied by Charles Lee and his family near the mouth of the river.

On the eighteenth the family of Mr. Kinzie, together with the servants and clerks in his trading establishment, were placed on board of a boat of sufficient capacity to accommodate them all, and they thus took their departure from the scene of so many calamities. There were left in the vicinity only Ouilmette and his family, who were the sole inhabitants of Chicago until the arrival, sometime later, of a French trader named Du Pin, who took possession of the unoccupied Kinzie house and lived in it. The length of his stay is not recorded.

The Indians now began to realize the folly of breaking up a station which to them was an abundant source of supplies, where they could come and obtain ammunition, provisions and clothing in exchange for their furs. They would henceforth be obliged to depend upon the small resources of the St. Joseph trading post or travel to Detroit.

All this had been foreseen by the older and wiser men among them, but the hot-blooded young men of the tribes were intent on plunder and the ghastly trophies represented by the scalps of their victims, and they could not be restrained. There was now little inducement to visit the post at Chicago; consequently the great numbers that formerly assembled in the neighbourhood scattered to remote places and eked out a precarious existence by fishing and hunting.

The Indians also found that the friendship of the British was a poor dependence as compared with that of the Americans, who were the only governmental authority with whom they could make treaties, and through whom they could obtain recognition and satisfaction for their claims of territorial ownership.

The following episode has been relegated to this late portion of the narrative, as belonging more to the echoes of the battle on the lake shore than to the battle itself.

Mrs. Lee was one of the women taken by the Indians when her husband and son had been killed at the massacre, as already narrated. She had with her a daughter twelve years old and an infant. These were claimed by our old friend Black Partridge under the following circumstances: The daughter had been placed on horseback for the march and tied fast for fear she would slip off the saddle. When the action was at its height she was severely wounded by a musket ball; and the horse, becoming frightened, set off at a gallop. The girl was partly thrown off, but was held fast by the bands, and hung dangling until she was met by Black Partridge, who caught the horse and disengaged her from the saddle. The chief had known the family and was greatly attached to this little girl, whom he recognized at once.

On finding that she was so seriously wounded that she could not recover, and that, besides, she was suffering great agony, he put the finishing stroke to her at once with his tomahawk. He said afterwards that this was one of the hardest things he ever attempted to do, but that he did it because he could not bear to see her suffer.

Black Partridge then took the mother and her infant to his village on the Au Sable, where he became warmly attached to the former. The author of *Wau-Bun* relates:

So much so, that he wished to marry her; but as she very naturally objected, he treated her with the greatest respect and consideration.

He was not disposed to liberate her from captivity, however, hoping that in time he could prevail upon her to become his wife.

During the following winter the child became ill, and was not restored by ordinary cures. Black Partridge then offered to take the child to Chicago, where the French trader named Du Pin, who had arrived after the massacre, was then living in the Kinzie house, and obtain medical aid from him. Accordingly the child was warmly wrapped, and the chief carried his precious charge all the way in his arms.

Arriving at the residence of M. du Pin, he carefully placed the child on the floor. "What have you there?" asked the trader.

"A young raccoon, which I have brought you as a present," replied the chief. Then opening the pack, he displayed the little sick child. M. du Pin furnished some remedies for its complaint and when Black Partridge was about to return he told the trader of his proposal to Mrs. Lee to become his wife, and of the way it had been received.

The *Wau-Bun* account, continues:

M. du Pin, being a man of discernment entertained some fears, that the chief's honourable resolution might not hold out, to leave it to the lady herself whether to accept his addresses or not, so he entered at once into a nego-tiation for her ransom, and so effectually wrought upon the good feelings of Black Partridge that he consented to bring his fair prisoner at once to Chicago, that she might be restored to her friends.

Mrs. Lee accordingly was brought to Chicago and had an

opportunity of expressing her gratitude to the French trader who had, without having seen her or known her, rendered so important a service as paying a ransom for her return to civilization. In course of time this M. du Pin, who it seems was a man without a family when he came, proposed to Mrs. Lee himself, and, more fortunate than the dusky chieftain, he was accepted. The *Wau-Bun* account says:

> We only know that in process of time Mrs. Lee became Madame du Pin, and that they lived together in great happiness for many years after.

It is a relief, after narrating the events connected with the evacuation of Fort Dearborn and the massacre which followed it, to invite the reader's attention to this picture, as a contrast with the havoc and dismay of that dreadful day in August, 1812, when Chicago was left with but one white inhabitant, and he a renegade.

At St. Joseph the Kinzie family remained under the protection of Chief Topenebe and his band until the following November. They were then conducted to Detroit under the escort of trusty Indian friends, and delivered up as prisoners of war to the British. Soon after John Kinzie was paroled, though afterwards again taken into custody. At the end of the war he was finally released, and in 1816 he again became a resident of Chicago, when the second Fort Dearborn was built and occupied by a garrison of United States troops.

After the destruction of Fort Dearborn, Chicago ceased for a time to be a fit dwelling-place for white men and their families. It continued in this condition with but little change for the following four years, and then the troops came back. Meanwhile peace had been concluded between the two warring nations, treaties of peace and friendship had been made with various tribes of Indians, and a new era began.

During the winter succeeding the battle and massacre the only two residents of Chicago who were householders were Ouilmette and Du Pin. A pretty fair estimate may be made of the total population of the place, including the half-breed children of Ouilmette and the *engagés* and helpers in the employ of Du Pin. It is safe to say that the total number was not more than ten or twelve persons.

Bloody retribution overtook at least one of those among the savages who on the day of the massacre showed no mercy to his victims. This was a chief known as a deadly enemy of the whites and who bore the expressive name of Shavehead, because of his peculiar manner of tying up his scanty hair. Years afterwards Chief Shavehead was in company with a band of hunters in the Michigan woods; in the party was a white man who had formerly been a soldier at Fort Dearborn, and was one of the survivors of the battle on the lake shore.

At one of the campfires the chief, being of a boastful disposition, related, while under the influence of liquor, to those sitting about the campfire, the frightful tale concerning the events of that day, dwelling upon its horrors and boasting of his own deeds. He was not aware that one of the whites whom he had so fiercely assailed was at that moment listening to his braggart utterances. The old soldier, as he heard the tale, was maddened by the recall of the well-remembered scenes.

Toward nightfall the old savage departed alone in the direction of the forest. Silently the soldier with loaded rifle followed upon his steps. Others observed them as they passed out of sight into the shades of the forest. The soldier returned after a time to his companions, but Shavehead was never again seen. "He had paid the penalty of the crime," says Mason, "to one who could with some fitness exact it."

The war of 1812, between the United States and Great Britain, was actually begun some time before the date of the declaration of war issued by the United States, on June 18, 1812; and it was continued some time after the treaty of peace had been signed, December 24, 1814. Of this war, the Fort Dearborn massacre on August 15, 1812, was one of the disastrous events.

Larned says:

The lives of thirty thousand Americans were sacrificed

during this war of two and a half years, and the national debt was increased one hundred millions of dollars.

Nine years cover the period of existence of Old Fort Dearborn. In that nine years of history it witnessed the efforts of three nations to subdue a continent, and played its part in the struggles between those nations. Established as a frontier post, it became an important link in the chain of western defences, and one of those schools of military instruction in which lessons were learned by those who had the task of preserving by force of arms a young republic in the midst of powerful and unscrupulous foes. A rallying point for traders and settlers in the virgin fields of the west, it was representative of a phase of development of the great Northwest Territory, and indeed of the development of the United States.

Its culminating disaster, which left it a heap of ruins, was one of those temporary setbacks which do not for long hold back the progress of such a growing nation. Within four years after the accident of war had made the fort and those in and about it the victims of a lingering barbarism, the foothold of the nation was secure in the west, the beginnings of its agricultural and commercial prosperity were laid, and upon the ruins of the old fort rose the walls of a new Fort Dearborn.